NO MAN CAN A-HINDER ME

A MESSAGE OF DEFIANCE FROM MY PLANTATION MOTHERS AND FATHERS

EDWARD W. ROBINSON, JR.

WITH

FREDERICK L. BONAPARTE

I wish to dedicate this book to great-great-great grandmother Nzinga, whose psychic spirit powered her kidnapper's ship to land in Trenton, New Jersey, in 1813 so that the story of who we are would not be lost; and to her great-grand daughter, Mary Anna Russell, who not only passed on the story to me, but taught me by example how to love unconditionally my family and my race; and to my immediate forbearers, whose marriages, for a century and a half, set the example "until death us do part."

E.W. Robinson, Jr.

ACKNOWLEDGEMENTS

No one has ever completed an important work by himself. Only the support and inspiration of those around him make a writer's work possible.

To my wife, Harriette, the heart and soul of this endeavor; to Fred Bonaparte, who insisted that I write this as a platform for the production of a series of motion pictures and whose writing skills and expert suggestions made a joy of a challenging undertaking; to Bob Lott who, with his great computer expertise, was of tremendous inspiration; to my daughters, Pam and Mickie, who gave me the "juice" to "keep on keeping on" and the scores of patient hearers of my message who inspired me with these words, "I don't remember everything you said, but I'll never forget how good you made me feel ."

I thank you for helping me to attempt to open the pathway to Black psychological freedom.

Edward W. Robinson, Jr., J.D., LL.D.

FOREWORD

Every February, vexing questions confront America and the world. Why do White people hold in contempt a race that has produced such brilliant, talented, creative and respected role models as President Barrack and First Lady Michele Obama, Jackie Robinson, Harriet Tubman, Oprah Winfrey, Gen. Colin Powell, Quincy Jones, Justice Thurgood Marshall, Dr. Martin Luther King, Marian Anderson, Dr. Mayou Angelo, Dr. George Washington Carver, Dr. William "Bill" Cosby and Ambassador Condoleeza Rice?

Why are the descendants of kings, queens, dynasties' pharaohs and pyramid builders killing each other, failing in school, enriching the penal system, populating poverty rolls and suffering a myriad of physical and mental ills in disproportionate numbers?

Why are contemporaries of Spike Lee, Mary J. Blige, Beyonce`, John Legend and Stevie Wonder lounging on the corners of our cities and towns with their pants on the ground and their caps turned around?

Why are White families fearful and move far away to houses they can't afford when a Black family moves next door, even if the Black family is headed by a doctor, lawyer or bank president?

Why does the myth that the Emancipation Proclamation "freed the (so-called) slaves" persist after almost 200 years?

This is my 93-year story of *why the answer to these questions can't be found in an annual parade of personalities during the month of February.*

I hope my experiences will assist White people to a better understanding of why they feel the way they do about Black people in spite of Black History Month's best efforts.

Also, I hope my experiences will assist Black people on the road to total freedom through emotional and historical reconditioning.

Edward W. Robinson, Jr., J.D., L.L.D.

NO MAN CAN A-HINDER ME

But now the days grow short,
I'm in the autumn of the year,
And now I think of my life as vintage wine
From fine old kegs
From the brim to the dregs
And it poured sweet and clear,
It was a very good year.

Every time I hear those words penned by Ervin Drake and sung by Frank Sinatra, I think: "Damn right, you had some 'very good years', Frank. You were White, wealthy, with a rich Italian heritage, a silky baritone voice and beautiful women at your beck and call. Go on and sing your song, "canti, il mio amico!"

It was not a very good year for people of African descent in 1918, the year I was born in Philadelphia, Pa. Despite the cries of delight when my parents, Ethel and Edward Wesley Robinson, Sr., welcomed my birth, a deadly flue epidemic ravaged the city in the fall of that year. Racial injustice plagued Black folks in almost every segment of their lives and the Great Depression of 1929 was just around the corner.

My family lived on Edwin Street, in a tiny row house in the Francesville section of the city. My mother and father could not have dreamed their first born would eventually earn a doctorate degree in law from Temple University, located just a few blocks away; or the infant delivered in their bedroom would one day be assistant to the mayor of Philadelphia; or their dimpled darling would much later be appointed a member of the board of direc- tors of the Philadelphia Federal Reserve Bank; or the diapers they changed were pinned around the bottom of a future presi- dent of a multi-million dollar insurance company... but I'm get- ting ahead of my 93-year-old story. Let's start at the beginning.

TABLE OF CONTENTS

EPILOGUE

TAKING OFFICE: Edward W. Robinson, Jr. (left),
is sworn in by Secretary of the Commonwealth of
Pennsylvania, Dr. C. DeLores Tucker and commissioned
by the Governor of Pennsylvania, Milton Shapp, as
Executive Deputy Secretary of the Commonwealth on
November 1, 1977.

CHAPTER ONE
The Beginning

My father, Edward Sr., was majestic in his features and as multi-talented as any man I have ever known. Although his skin color was as richly pigmented as chestnuts roasting on an open fire, he had blue eyes and curly hair. His formal education ended at sixth grade, but he astounded customers at the plumbing supply where he worked by solving piping problems that required a thorough knowledge of higher mathematics. My mother, Ethel, fitted the traditional mode of the well-educated woman of the day. Her color was, as my father described it, "sweet potato pie brown". She was a graduate of Girl's High School, which to this day is considered one of the country's premier educational institutes. She majored in music at the University of Pennsylvania, which enrolled only a handful of African origin students at that time. Articulate and graceful, she taught piano and organ lessons.

John Robinson, my paternal grandfather, was poorly pigmented (light-skinned), with straight hair and light eyes. His family lived on a farm in West Maryland, but when we asked where he was from originally, he always changed the subject. Grandmother Robinson, his wife, said he wouldn't divulge his birthplace, but our research uncovered events of racial brutality.

We believed grandfather Robinson was the child of a White man who raped my great grandmother, a common violation during our captivity. We also believe grandfather Robinson escaped after committing assault on a White man and was advised he would be hunted down and murdered if his whereabouts were revealed.

My maternal grandfather, Alfred Russell, was also a child born out of the rape of a Black woman by a White man. His mother told him the gruesome story of how she was held down by two overseers as the plantation owner viciously beat her into submission. She admonished Grandfather Russell to never forget how he was conceived and to never let his children or grandchildren forget the crime.

Grandfather Russell and his wife, Mary Anna, lived two doors down the street from my house. If there ever was a child who was the "apple of grandmother's eye," I must have been the whole fruit basket. I was, truly, the star in her crown. The legacy that my grandparents left with me was unconditional love for my children, their children and each succeeding generation.

Another legacy gift I received from the Russells was their sensitivity to community need. Although their household funds were meager, Mary Anna and Alfred canvassed the neighborhood for food, funds and other necessities during the holidays for the less fortunate families in the neighborhood. During the summer, Alfred, who made a little money hauling furniture and household goods, frequently loaded neighbors on his small truck for outings in Fairmount Park, several miles from Edwin St.

In addition to my grandfather Alfred's community outreach, he was, along with my father, tremendously protective of me. I experienced this in most memorable ways.

EDWARD W. ROBINSON, SR. My father, who retired from the huge pipe-supply Hajoca Corporation after 40 years, was told by the president, "With your knowledge of pipe-fitting and your expertise in creating blue prints, we would have made you manager of the whole shop if you were White." An excellent boxer and athlete, Dad managed the neighborhood uniformed teenage teams and never tired of giving quality time to his children,

ETHEL MATHILDA ROBINSON, my MOTHER, played the piano and organ at our church, gave music lessons at home and accompanied me in my small concerts on the violin. When I graduated from college with seven grades of A+ and one A, she demanded to know what happened to the other A+. She was not happy with the blonde color of my sister's hair and unsuccessfully tried to darken it with frequent rinses of dark tea water.

ALFRED RUSSELL. My maternal grandfather, was the quiet, neighborhood piano-lifting strong man. He never got over his anger about how his mother was raped by his Maryland plantation owner White father. A self-employed furniture mover all his life, Russell couldn't understand how people could be unemployed, even during the Depression.

MARY ANNA RUSSELL. I could do no wrong in the eyes of my maternal grandmother. When I clumsily fell down in a stage play, she excitedly jumped to her feet and directed the audience to "Watch how gracefully he gets up!" A church organist and neighborhood politician, she was was born in Philadelphia, Pa. and graduated from the school which was later known as Cheyney State College.

MARY DIANE THOMAS, my great- grandmother, loved telling the story of her grandmother, Nzinga. She described how Nzinga looked and her life in Benin City, Nigeria. Grandmother Thomas, who transitioned at 89 when I was 13, also praised her husband, John, who was born in Haddonfield, New Jersey. They migrated to Philadelphia, Pa. in 1865.

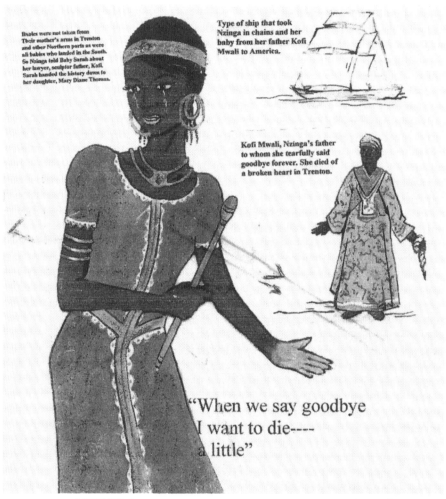

Babies were not taken from Their mother's arms in Trenton and other Northern ports as were all babies who landed in the South. So Nzinga told Baby Sarah about her lawyer, sculptor father, Kofi. Sarah handed the history down to her daughter, Mary Diane Thomas.

Type of ship that took Nzinga in chains and her baby from her father Kofi Mwali to America.

Kofi Mwali, Nzinga's father to whom she tearfully said goodbye forever. She died of a broken heart in Trenton.

"When we say goodbye
I want to die----
a little"

NZINGA, my great-great-great-grandmother, whose name meant "beautiful," was born and raised in Benin City, Nigeria. She was married to my great-great-great grandfather, Konata (Nobleman) Mwali, a lawyer and sculptor. His work was probably part of the thousands of art treasure stolen by England from Nigeria. (See *Treasures of Ancient Nigeria,* by Ekpo Eyo and Frank Willett, published by Knopf, New York, 1980). This artist rendition, described to me by great-grandmother Mary Diane Thomas, shows Nzinga's tears of sorrow at being taken by force from her beloved African home.

CHAPTER TWO
My Mentors

My father and grandfather Alfred were my examples of strong, responsible manhood.

Edwin St. was an oasis in the middle of an area populated by hostile Whites. Caution was my companion on the way home, to school and to my newspaper delivery route. One day I was accosted by a large, teenage White bully who demanded to know "What business a nigger had delivering papers in a White neighborhood". I knew I would have to fight. I was only 10 or 11 years old, so I asked the bully to send out his brother, who was about my age, to fight for the family racial honor.

My father had taught me to box and, using my advantage as a southpaw (left-handed), I proceeded to beat the Caucasian out of the little brother. His mother, hearing the fray, grabbed an umbrella and stormed outside, beating me on the head, swearing and talking about my ancestry in a most vulgar way.

Bleeding, I went home to tell my father, who raced to the offending house and challenged EVERYBODY to come outside. The last I heard, the whole family packed up and moved to parts unknown.

Ridge Avenue, a hodge-podge of small businesses, bordered my neighborhood and extended all the way to the northern suburbs of the city. The Ridge Ave. Theatre, a segregated movie house, was within walking distance of my house. Black people sat on the left and White people sat on the right, where they had a clearer view of the screen. Being a bit of a rebel, I decided one day to sit on the "White side." The manager was summoned and he roughly lifted me by my shirt collar and planted me in a seat on the 'Black side'.

When grandfather Alfred came home from work and heard the story, he led a couple of his moving helpers around the corner to the movie house. Grandfather was a piano mover. He could lift one end of the instrument while it took two men to grasp the other side. Legend has it that grandfather was so strong, he once knocked a horse down with a single blow!

Grandfather entered the theatre and brushed past the cashier without paying as she screamed for help.

When the manager rushed out of his office, grandfather, without a word, grabbed the startled White man by the collar and slammed him up against the wall so hard, plaster fell like winter snow.

"Is this the man?" grandfather demanded.

"Yes sir", I replied.

"My grandson can sit anywhere he chooses, do you understand?" my grandfather hissed through clenched teeth, his grip tightening around the man's collar.

"Yes sir," the frightened manager replied.

And I sat wherever I chose from that day forward, with later apologies to Dr. Martin Luther King. Nobody had come along at that time to teach grandfather Alfred the righteousness of nonviolence.

These and many other incidents of protection served to create a shield around my ego, warding off many racist assaults in my early school life.

CHAPTER THREE
My Siblings

I remember feeling very protective of my brother, Calvin, who was born when I was five and my sister, Elaine, who was born five years later. I also recall wanting to protect Elaine from the moment I first saw her. Her foot-long hair looked like corn silk around her cherubic little face.

The unselfish side of Calvin was clearly evident at an early age as he shared his toys and clothing with children in the neighborhood who were less fortunate. Calvin also had a reputation for getting into scrapes with older, larger boys and running home imploring me to "get" his tormentors. Fortunately, my southpaw boxing style again came to our rescue against untrained opponents. Calvin's unselfish side resurfaced in later years as he committed himself to the Black community by providing vital economic and historic guidance.

Elaine played the "baby sister" role to the hilt. Calvin and I provided protection for her from birth to her courtship days, "checking out" the young men who came seeking her hand.

While pursuing a career as an educator, she married and had a daughter, Elaine II, who tragically died at 18.

Elaine's crowning achievement was that she became the mother of State Legislator David P. Richardson, who went on to national fame as an up-and-coming civil rights fighter and might have become the next

Pennsylvania congressman had his life not been cut short by a serious illness at the height of his career.

MY SISTER, BROTHER AND I: I was 24, Elaine
(left), was 13 and Calvin, (center), was 18 in this 1941
photo. I was attending University of Pennsylvania
graduate school while working for an insurance
company, earning $30-per-week as an agent. Calvin and
I later co-authored *Journey of the Songhai People*. My
brother was also active in the testing of three thousand
young people who were taken to Africa, free of charge,
by a group called the D'Zert Club. Elaine went on to
become a school teacher.

CHAPTER FOUR
Elementary School

I attended Lydia Darrah Elementary School at 17th & Folsom Sts., within walking distance of my house. The student population was 90% White and the teachers and administration were 99% racist. Educational expectations for White students were as high as the North Star and, for the Black students, as low as whale excrement, which is found at the bottom of the ocean.

Teachers frequently deplored our "low learning ability" and I was told by Mrs. Rothman, my 8th grade teacher, that I "didn't have enough intelligence to go on to Central High School".

Central, a school that included junior and senior high grades, was noted as the top public school of its kind in the country.

Mrs. Rothman was angry with me because I raised my hand to answer literally every question she asked the class. When she refused to call on me, I pretended inattention and when she purposely called my name, I embarrassed her with the correct answer.

The adulation of poorly pigmented skin color and the rejection of rich pigmentation permeated every corner of the school. It was not unusual for my cousin, who had long hair and a coffee-with-cream complexion, to be told by White teachers, "You're pretty, for a colored girl".

The "worship of white" even included some churches. After my grandmother, Mary, visited 1st African Baptist Church at 16th and Christian Sts., she came home broken-hearted because she was barred from sitting with her close, but lightly pigmented friend.

"You will have to sit in the balcony," my dark chocolate grandmother was told firmly by the poorly pigmented usher on the door.

"But that's my friend and we came together," my grandmother protested."

" She can sit downstairs, but the balcony is for the colored" came the impatient reply.

Also, ushers at two West Philadelphia Presbyterian churches tried to discourage attendance of worshipers with "skin darker than a paper bag".I hate to think what will happen when those ushers find out that all the gate keepers in Heaven "don't like ugly!"

Not only did Philadelphia harbored racial hostility in theatres, schools and churches, but in many other places in the 1930s. My feelings were bruised at many of these establishments.

CHAPTER FIVE
My Neighborhood

There was a White Castle restaurant on Ridge Ave., near the theatre. A large sign in the window announced 'White trade solicited only'.

When my mother explained what 'solicited' meant, the future direction of my life as a foe of racism began to take form at 13-years-old.

Lest I forget, a counselor at Darrah, noticing my husky stature, advised me to forget the pursuit of a college education and seek work as a laborer. Despite the racial animosity of my teachers, counselors and neighborhood, I was accepted at Central and graduated 4th in my class with honors and a bachelors degree. I hurried back to Darrah Elementary School to show Mrs. Rothman my accomplishments, but her eyes, dimmed by denial of African intelligence, were rendered semi-sightless.I began to wonder: Why is there so much hostility against us Black people?

CHAPTER SIX
The Tarzan Lie

It is estimated that 95% of African Americans do not know the country of their origin. Of that group, 90% are quick to dispute or disregard any connection to the Motherland. Why?

Because America and the rest of the world has been conditioned to believe that Africa is a savage jungle overrun by lions, tigers and other wild beasts. We are taught that Africa is an extremely dangerous country where small, richly pigmented people regularly dance and sing while they boil strangers in big pots over open fires. These uneducated, unchurched, diaper-wearing natives would probably be extinct today if they hadn't been rescued by a tall, White, tree-swinging saviour named Tarzan. He was often accompanied on his mercy missions by a dark haired, voluptuous woman named Jane and a little chimpanzee, whose name I forget.

Tarzan, a mythical cartoon character created by Edgar Rice Burroughs, was carried in most major newspapers around the world. Burroughs, who had never been to Africa, helped to propagate a poisonous attitude toward anything African, a profitable strategy created by European captors to justify our captivity.

Unfortunately, "Tarzanization" is alive and well today, causing low racial esteem among people of color and an unhealthy, false feeling of superiority among people with less pigmentation. Fortunately, my family shielded me from "Tarzanization" by sharing with me the wonderful stories of my Nigerian ancestors.

CHAPTER SEVEN
My Roots

I was protected from "Tarzanization" by stories of my African family learned at the knee of my maternal great grandmother, Mary Diane Thomas. Mrs. Thomas, who resided two doors down the street with my grandmother, Mary Russell, lived until I was 13-years-old and never tired of telling me of our Nigerian ancestry.

She was the grand daughter of Nzinga and Kudjo Mwali, who lived in Benin City, Nigeria in the early 1800s. Benin was a beautiful city of universities, porched homes, paved streets, quaint shops and indoor plumbing.

Great-great-great grandfather Kudjo, who was a lawyer and sculptor, was infuriated because British soldiers continually came to the city and stole art treasures, including sculptures, from the Benin cultural centers. Kudjo and Nzinga often argued over Kudjo's vow to fight the soldiers on their next plundering visit. Nzinga's anxiety was heightened by the fact she was pregnant and she feared her husband might be killed.

Despite her pleas, Kudjo rallied his fellow sculptors and, sadly, was killed fighting British soldiers 1813.

Great-great-great grandmother Nzinga was captured with 247 Africans as prisoners-of-war and marched, chained neck-to-neck, many miles to a Ghana port. There, they were boarded on an American so-called "slave ship" bound for Charleston, South Carolina. Enroute to America, the vessel was captured by an Abolitionist ship, which was enforcing a United States law of 1808 prohibiting importation of additional Africans. U.S shipping companies ignored the law because the illegal trafficking of Africans had become an incredible source of income.

The commandeered captive ship was rerouted to the port of Trenton, New Jersey. All of the captured Africans were adopted by various Abolitionist families.

Great-great-great grandmother Nzinga had given birth aboard ship to a girl she named Diane, who was my great-great grandmother. Mother and child were adopted by an Abolitionist couple with the family name of Stewart.

Since African families were not separated in the North as was the practice by Southern captors, Nzinga was able to pass on stories of Benin City to great -great grandmother Diane and the stories finally made their way to my eager ears on Edwin Street from great grandmother Mary Diane.

Thus, I was protected from the Tarzan lies and other insidious attempts to make us all believe African "jungle stories".

Incidentally, there was a tour (1980) of Nigerian sculpture presented at the Art Museum in Philadelphia, which is a short walk from Edwin Street. It would not surprise me if some of my great-great-great grandfather's work is finally being enjoyed around the world.

Discovering that I came from African greatness excited me. On the preceding pages are pictures of my ancestors which, along with the illustrations of Songhai, motivated me through the years to share them with the world.

CHAPTER EIGHT
My First Sit-in

Edward K. Nichols, who later became an army officer, lawyer and pastor, was the valedictorian of my Central High graduating class.

In 1935 the country was in the midst of the Depression and Nichols and I joined the city-wide search for a free college education. Philadelphia Normal School For Teachers offered an undergraduate course with free tuition and books, but only high school seniors who had a grade point average of 90 or above could apply for the 75 openings. I was accepted at Philadelphia Normal School, despite Mrs. Rothman's bias-tinged prediction, and Nichols went on to Howard University.

A drug store, at Ridge and Girard Avenues, would accept your money for take-out purchases, but reserved the soda fountain area for White trade. There were no signs, just menacing glares and no service if you dared sit at the counter.

Remembering the grandfather Alfred incident years earlier, just two blocks down the street, Nichols and I decided to sit at the fountain. It was a hot day and the ice cream sodas in front of the White patrons looked mighty tempting. As we moved toward the fountain, the counterman came over, planted his face close to ours and told us whom the seats were reserved for. We planted our posteriors on the revolving stools and ordered French vanilla sundaes with hot chocolate fudge.

The counterman tried the standard tactic of ignoring us, but the longer we sat, discussing the news of the day, the larger the crowd grew surrounding us. Finally, fearing the unknown, the counterman served us. But we left the sundaes untouched, in case poison had been discreetly added.

Outside, on the pavement, Ed and I would have high-fived each other, but that sign of accomplishment was still 50 years away. So we laughed, hugged and strode away in victory.

I went on to Philadelphia Normal School, which had supplied teachers to Philadelphia schools for 120 years. Fortunately, the buffering of my ego by my family enabled me to withstand the many rough experiences at Philadelphia Normal School.

CHAPTER NINE
Faculty Disrespect

There were many bumps in the racial road at Philadelphia Normal School despite the excellent academic education I received.

There was another student in my class with the surname Robinson and the all-White faculty pretended to not be able to tell us apart. It made no difference that I was taller and poorly pigmented (light) and he was short and richly pigmented (dark). There was a cleaning powder advertised during that time called "The Gold Dust Twins". On the front of the box was the caricature of two African boys, complete with bulging eyes, thick red lips and bones in their noses. The faculty thought it great fun to disrespect us and the "Gold Dust Twins" label followed us throughout our Normal School years. In 1937, one of the most embarrassing experiences of my life occurred when I was called a racial slur I had not heard before.

CHAPTER TEN
"White Nigger"

I loved soccer at Philadelphia Normal School and I was the star fullback on the team. I remember the initial meeting between our team and Girard College. Both teams were undefeated and city lovers of the sport waited excitedly for the title match.

There was one problem. Stephen Girard's will barred Black people from entering the gates, for sports, maintenance, entertainment or anything else.

Being poorly pigmented, my coach decided to have me 'pass' as a White player, but my hair was fully developed (thick, protective). We decided I would wear a close-fitting hat during the game. Going into a soccer game of city-wide importance without the star fullback was simply unacceptable.

Everything was going well and our team was kicking Girard's butt, literally and figuratively.

Suddenly, in a violent clash, my hat flew off. The stadium, after a second of shocked silence, rose as one and shouted repeatedly, "Get the white nigger!"

Security guards quickly rushed on the field and unceremoniously ushered me out the front gates for my safety.

Philadelphia Normal School refused to play without me and Girard College was forced to forfeit the game, the only loss on their schedule that season.

Philadelphia Normal finished the year undefeated.Racism at Philadelphia Normal tried to attack my ego in many activities, including classroom, sports, political and even social. There was one example of social racism that really taxed my understanding of White fear.

CHAPTER ELEVEN
Ms. Doyle's Revenge

The Philadelphia Normal School ban on interracial fraternization between Black and White students was both stupid and ludicrous.

Each month a student dance was held in the gymnasium and teachers were assigned to enforce the no-mixing rule. The waltz between a richly pigmented brother and a poorly pigmented sister was rudely interrupted by a hawk-eyed teacher who thought the sister was White. Despite his protests, the brother was ushered off the floor, hustled to the principal's office and immediately suspended. Believe it or not, *the sister had to bring her parents to school to prove she was Black* before the brother was readmitted. Needless to say, there were no apologies offered to either student.

I was active in athletics, a straight A student, violinist in the school orchestra and genuinely enjoyed by my fellow students. So it wasn't a surprise when my peers overwhelmingly voted me to be president of the Student Association. As soon as the election results were known, I was summoned into the office of Florence A. Doyle, principal of the school.

Expecting to be congratulated, I was flabbergasted when Ms. Doyle warned me not to take the top student post.

"Why not?" I asked her.

"In the 125 years of this school's existence, there has never been a negro president", she replied.

"So what?" I replied.

"As president you'll be interacting with White girls and that is forbidden. I will expect your resignation on my desk by tomorrow".

At home, my parents told me to ignore the principal. When Ms. Doyle's demand was rejected, she warned me, "You will regret this!"

Philadelphia Normal was a teaching school and each student was required to pass subjective practice teaching evaluations, starting in the second year.

The regular teacher would sit in the back of the class to keep an eye on the students and the evaluator would observe the skills of the practice teacher.

By some strange coincidence, every regular teacher of my practice classes called in sick on the day I was scheduled. As a consequence, the evaluator automatically gave me less than a passing grade.

"I told you I'd get even," Ms. Doyle said gleefully as she posted a flunking practice teaching grade next to my A's in every other subject.

The horrific irony of this small-minded administrator's act of revenge is that, in later years, I went on to teach members of the Board of Education, students, principals, counselors, teachers and education administrators.

But Ms. Doyle had the last word. Her rejection of me as a human being, strictly because of the color of my skin,caused me to develop a bleeding ulcer which is a source of discomfort I still feel 76 years later.

As I have indicated before, there were many White humanists. We have heard of and even sang about John Brown, perhaps the most outstanding White foe of Black injustice.

CHAPTER TWELVE
Girard College Disgrace

John Brown's body lies a'mouldering in the grave,
John Brown's body lies a'mouldering in the grave,
John Brown's body lies a'mouldering in the grave,
His truth is marching on!

You've probably heard the poem, sung to the tune of the Battle Hymn Of The Republic, many times. John Brown was a White abolitionist who was hanged in 1859 because his 'truth' was the fight against enslavement of African people.

Stephen Girard, born in France in 1750, had a diametrically opposed "truth." Girard believed that African people should be captured and treated as property, i.e. sold, bought, traded, abused and separated from families totally at the convenience of their White captors.

Why do I bring this up?

Girard College is a huge, 45-acre campus two blocks from the old Ridge Ave. Theatre and six blocks from my birthplace. Serving students starting in elementary grades, the College and boarding school was built and financed with millions provided in the will of the same

Steven Girard who engaged in, profited from and tried to perpetuate racial segregation even after his death.Acknowledged during his lifetime as the richest man in America, Girard amassed an immense fortune in shipping, construction, banking, coal mining and railroads.

Not so well known is the initial source of much of his wealth. History buffs claim that Girard, through his shipping interests in the Caribbean, met Toussaint L'Ouverture, ruler of Haiti, at the beginning of the 19ᵗʰ century. Fresh from leading a victorious Haitian army against Napoleon and the French army and navy, L'Ouverture was invited to France to debate the war to free African captives in the Caribbean. Fearing a ruse, L'Ouverture, in his *Memoirs**, mentions that he sent "six million francs to Stephen Girard" in Philadelphia to purchase "weapons and ammunition". The money "was misappropriated" according to Girard employees. L'Ouverture died in an Alps prison, tricked by Napoleon.

A biographer of the day reported that Girard, on at least one occasion, shipped "a cargo of niggers" to a Philadelphia port.

It is not well known that Girard owned Africans on his Mount Holly, New Jersey farm for more than 50 years.

It is a matter of record that his 1848 "irrevocable will" specifically prohibited people of African descent, females, priests and clergymen from entering the grounds of Girard College.

Decades of legal assaults on the will were argued By attorneys William Coleman and Raymond Pace Alexander.

Years of protest marches around the 10-foot high stone walls of the College were led by NAACP attorney Cecil Moore, Dr. Martin Luther King and other civil rights leaders. Finally, the walls of segregation at Girard College came tumbling down in 1968 .

As I look at the computer home page of Girard College in the year 2011, I see beautiful African and Asian boys and girls on campus playing, studying and enjoying themselves. Stephen Girard's ghost has surely tried to angrily crack every stone in Founder's Hall as a gorgeous African American queen, Dr. Autumn Adkins Graves, today provides world-class leadership as

Girard College president!

Glory, glory hallelujah,
Jim Crow's lies ain't marching on!

---

* Schiller report: "The United States Debt to Haiti" by Carlos Wesley.

PROTESTORS OF RACISM around the Girard College walls were joined by civil rights groups, churches, unions, students, fraternities, sororities and people from around the country in this 1967 photo. John Lewis, who went on to become a Georgia congressman, was a young participant in this demonstration.

CHAPTER THIRTEEN
Beauty & The Campus

Florence Doyle's racist revenge created within me a guarded caution around White people that elicited instant creative retorts to White insults.

For example: After being accepted for enrollment at Virginia State College For Negroes, I journeyed to the institution to begin my education there. Stepping off the train in Petersburg, Va., I was hailed by a White traveler.

"Say, George" he called. "How do you find Halifax Street?"

"What makes you think my name is George?" I asked.

"I just guessed it," the man replied.

"Well, keep on guessing until you find Halifax St." I shot back, leaving the man perplexed by my unexpected, irritated response.

Hailing a taxicab driven by a friendly Black driver, I settled in the back seat with my luggage and excitedly envisioned my new life at Virginia State College For Negroes (the designation "For Negroes" was dropped shortly after I enrolled).

This was to be my first "down South" experience. I had been warned that neither Constitutional law, Biblical love or man's humanity to man had any meaning for southern Whites in their treatment and regard of African Americans.

But I had survived, with the help of my family, painful thorns of racial injustice "up South" at Darrah Elementary, Central High and Philadelphia Normal School. Despite being a straight A student, I was rarely acknowledged as more than a "husky colored boy" during my Philadelphia educational years.

I mentally put on my African helmet and , in today's film hero terms, prepared to "do a Denzel Washington" if faced with racial adversity.

As the taxi rounded a curve in the road and Virginia State College came into view, I was awe-struck by the beauty of the buildings surrounded by lush foliage. Having endured 17 years of Philadelphia bricks and grey cement, the initial sighting of the next step in my life experience took my breath away!

The information I had gleaned from my college search hailed Virginia State as tops among Historically Black Colleges. The reports ranked Virginia State first in academics, the arts, basketball, track and football.

But what particularly intrigued me was the report of the most beautiful young ladies on earth occupying the Virginia State dormitories. Academics, sports and music were and are very important to me, but the vision of wave after wave of gorgeous queens washing up on the beach of my 17-year-old libido made it imperative that Virginia State be my first choice. Incidentally, when I enrolled, the ratio of students was 660 girls to 400 boys!

That last piece of valuable information was passed on to me by John Carter, a best friend from Philadelphia. John, who enrolled at Virginia State a year before me, met me at the gate with an enthusiastic bear hug. "Let's get some food first and then I'll take you on a tour of the campus," he promised.

I was so hungry, I could have eaten my luggage, so I tagged along behind John to a large cafeteria that wafted smells so tempting, they brought tears to my eyes.

The standard meal at the Philadelphia Normal School cafeteria was usually potatoes, a sturdy vegetable like broccoli, asparagus or green beans and some kind of beef covered with an unappetizing gravy.

At Virginia State, expert hands had prepared a menu of scrumptious macaroni and cheese, tasty collard greens, candied yams, fluffy homemade biscuits, lip-smacking fried chicken, fresh fruit and ice cold lemonade. Cuisine for queens and kings! While my mouth enjoyed the royal buffet, my eyes wandered around the cafeteria, feasting on a bevy of the most beautiful young women I had ever seen.

John, in all his descriptions, had failed to do justice to the female flower garden of Virginia State College. Every color, from the dark chocolate brown of sun-ripened coffee beans down to the blush pink of ripened peaches on a California vine was represented. Their hair, shapes, demeanors and styles were fashion-book excellent.

Noting I seemed immobilized by so much so soon, John assured me that he would arrange a meeting with some of the young ladies after the lunch period. Now, that's what friends are for!

Before the end of my first day at Virginia State, Philadelphia's Ms. Doyle, Ms. Rothman, the Ridge Ave. Theatre manager and others of their racist ilk seemed light years away.

After my exhilarating first day, I couldn't believe that I would face even more excitement in the days ahead.

CHAPTER FOURTEEN
Educational Revelations

I can't describe the awesome feeling I experienced as I met my brilliant and skilled professors, all African Americans. It was my first experience, in 15 years of schooling, that I had the privilege of being taught by Black faculty members. The positive, loving nurturing I received from my Virginia State teachers was the exact opposite of the scorn, ridicule and low expectations heaped upon my ego in Philadelphia schools.

One of the most powerful influences of my college life was George Singleton, head of the Department of Business as well as my accounting teacher. His teaching led me to believe the lack of an economic base was the reason for the negative treatment of Black people by Whites. Under his tutelage, I changed my major from education to business administration. Fueled by his enthusiasm and wisdom, I quickly became a straight-A student. While still in my teens, I vowed to do all in my power to rescue my people from ignominious failure by advocating positive economics. I fully believed that once we achieved financial stability, the veil of White disrespect would be lifted.

Little did I know I had much to learn!

Professor J. Harold Montague, who was so skillful he could draw beautiful sounds from rocks, was the premier director of the Virginia State choir and glee club. The "Angelic Choir" was so successful, it was in constant demand to perform in concert at other colleges and cities. I was chosen for the glee club and choir after an audition and Professor Montague became a dominate influence in my musical life.

Another major player in my future destiny was Dr. Luther P. Jackson, my history teacher. Professor Jackson constantly drummed into my head; "You must tell the story of our ancestors, the Songhai people." He also insisted that I visit the Schomburg Collection in New York City, one of the most extensive libraries and collections of African art and artifacts in America.

The story of how the Collection came to be is interesting. Arturo Schomburg, born in Puerto Rico, was the son of wealthy parents, his mother African, his father Jewish. Schomburg attended the finest private schools and made a habit of winning every scholarship award that came up for contest. The school's administrators and his fellow students were quick to credit his brilliance to "the 50% White blood in his veins." He was equally quick to reply, "If 50% White blood is so special, why do you people with 100% White blood not score higher than I do?" While they searched for a reply, Schomberg provided the answer. "Logically it must be my African blood that propels me to the top."

Schomburg vowed to tell the true story of his African heritage and the Schomburg Collection was born.

As part of my continuing education, I have tried to spend a part of each summer at the Collection site in New York learning more of our history.

Thank you, Brother Schomburg!

However, I want to hold up some other notables among my Virginia State colleagues.

CHAPTER FIFTEEN
Celebrity Breeding Ground

The list of celebrities and other notables who graduate from Historically Black Colleges and Universities (HBCU's) is long and distinguished.   A little-known study revealed that only 20% of Black college graduates in America attended HBCUs.   However, 80% of African American leaders and luminaries came from that tiny 20%.   The analysis gave credit to the nurturing atmosphere created by caring, creative Black administrators and faculty.

I was a benefactor of that nurturing and so were the following classmates and friends that I recall with pride and admiration:

Dr. Billy Taylor, jazz pianist, composer, broadcaster and educator, qualities that made him one of America's most cherished national treasures.   Dr. Taylor, whose recording career spanned over six decades, composed over three hundred and fifty songs, as well as works for theatre, dance and symphony orchestras.

Virginia State students remember how he mesmerized us many afternoons in the College conservatory with his jazz piano artistry. Dr. Taylor died in December, 2010.

Camillla Williams, world- celebrated soprano, the first African American singer to sing the title role of Puccini's *Madama Butterfly* with the New York City Opera in 1946. Ms. Williams scored another first in 1954 when she sang the major role of *Cio-Cio-San* with the Vienna State Opera in 1954. More on this internationally acclaimed diva later.

The Jordans (not their real name), were a brother and sister whose mother acquired a sizeable nest egg for their education by using good old African ingenuity.

Ms. Jordan, an attractive single mother, worked for a wealthy White family as a live-in employee for many years. A dedicated worker, Ms. Jordan was aware the White family owned a very large business. When offered wage increases, Ms. Jordan, instead, wisely asked for and received "little pieces of paper with the corporation name at the top."

When the value of the company skyrocketed because of the demands of World War II, Ms. Jordan unlocked her strongbox to check out its contents. She rebuffed company efforts to purchase the contents and cashed in her "little pieces of paper" (stock certificates) to provide a worry-free retirement for herself and a comfortable campus life for her children at Virginia State College.

William J. Kennedy III was the son of the president of North Carolina Mutual Insurance Company, the largest Black-owned corporation in America. Kennedy III eventually became president of the corporation headquartered in Durham, North Carolina and, years later, I became a vice president.

Joe Hall, a premier football and track star, became an entrepreneur after graduation. He also served a stint as a Philadelphia police detective. Hall was best known as the owner of the *Postal Card ,* a South Street restaurant and nightspot, which was a must-visit mecca for jazz-loving Philadelphians and tourists alike. He and his wife, Ercelle, a former high-ranking government official, are the parents of educator, poet, playwright Joee Hall-Hoxter and Evelyn Wells, an international expert on education.

Every member of the Hall family is a Virginia State graduate. *John Borican,* international track star-artist, who set Penn Relay record for 1500 meters that lasted 25 years, was a football and academic standout and supremely self-confident.

When I was introduced to him, he said,

"Congratulations!"

"For what?' I asked.

'You are shaking hands with the great me," he explained with clarion sincerity.

His artistry with oils and easel easily matched his feats in football, track or the classroom. His portrait from a sketch of Dr. John Gandy, president of Virginia State College, looked so life-like, it could have walked off the canvas. After graduation, he opened an art studio in New York City.Tragically, he died of leukemia at 29.

Comparing the joys my Virginia State years to my Philadelphia educational experience is like comparing champagne to greasy dishwater. Nurtured and enthusiastic, I graduated summa cum laude in 1940. The next event immediately set the direction of my life.

DR. BILLY TAYLOR is shown in this1974 photo discussing a musical score with famed singer Ella Fitzgerald during funeral services for bandleader Duke Ellington. A pianist, composer, arranger, author, lecturer and TV personality, Dr. Taylor earned a degree in music from Virginia State College in 1942. An international ambassador of jazz, Dr. Taylor died in 2010 at the age of 89.

CHAPTER SIXTEEN
Getting Down To Business

Diploma in hand, I was anxious to return to Philadelphia to use the knowledge and experience I had happily inhaled at Virginia State.

Remembering the admonition of Professor Singleton and the success of North Carolina Mutual, I formed a career battle plan. I would find a small insurance company in the telephone book, apply for a job and grow with the company until my million-dollar-plus dream was realized. I was still living rent-free with my parents on Edwin Street and if enthusiasm and the will to work was a qualification for success, look out world!

Insurance companies didn't come any smaller than Provident Home Industrial Mutual Insurance Company, a tiny south Philadelphia operation with a name longer than its assets. The company, in the 1700 block of Christian Street, shared a ramshackle building that had seen better days. I met the company president, Joseph A. Faison, in a basement meeting room that leaked from a toilet on an upper floor. Faison greeted this Virginia State, finance major, summa cum laude graduate with open arms. He immediately signed me on as an agent and, after a one-hour training orientation, sent me out on Christian Street to sell insurance door-to-door.

I was paid on commission only and I, as luck would have it, sold a policy to one of the first people to answer my ringing of their doorbell. My joy and expectations knew no bounds!

After the first week of pavement-pounding, I earned the magnificent commission of seventy five cents. But I would not be deterred. I could only see the challenge as an opportunity.

The other agents greeted my spirited efforts with scorn and derision when I celebrated the doubling of my commissions to one dollar and fifty cents the second week. My co-workers really fell on the floor laughing when I predicted Provident Home Mutual would one day be worth more than a million dollars!

I was driven with the passion of Professor Singleton's teaching as my commissions increased until I was able to save enough to buy an Essex car for fifty dollars.

Owning a car enabled me to travel around the city promoting insurance sales and promote concert events on the side. Through it all, I maintained a high level of enthusiasm, remembering the word enthusiasm means "God within."

Having "wheels" enabled me also to carry out a promise I had made to Camilla Williams, the songbird.

CHAPTER SEVENTEEN
The Promoter In Me

One of my most successful concerts as a part-time promoter was the introduction to Philadelphia of the Virginia State Choir featuring soprano Camilla Williams. It is an understatement to say the packed auditorium was awe-struck at the wondrous sound that came from the stage that evening. Ms. Williams' lyrical voice brought to mind the words of Paul Lawrence Dunbar's poem "The nightingales hush their mouths when my Lindy sings."

Seated in the audience was Maroin Szekely Freschl, a teacher at the Julliard School, who was also a mentor of world-acclaimed contralto Marian Anderson.

Ms. Freschl was so taken with Camilla's voice, she offered her a 7-year voice scholarship if she could come to Philadelphia.

I organized the Philadelphia Chapter of the Alumni Association of Virginia State College around the central theme of Camilla's career. The Association raised transportation money for Camilla and two Alumni members, Ashley and Helen Jones, offered Camilla living quarters for seven years while she studied.

In addition, Ashley, who was the projectionist at the Pearl movie theatre at 21st and Ridge Ave., secured an ushering job for the singer during the full term of her tutelage under Ms. Freschl.

Camilla went on to win the Marion Anderson Fellowship in 1943 and 1944, performed on the coast-to-coast RCA network, sang throughout the United States and Europe with major opera companies and was one of eight women honored by the Library of Virginia during Women's History Month in 2007. Ms. Williams retired as Professor of Voice at Indiana University in 1980.

The war temporarily sidetracked my trek to success and reminded me that racial injustice was still alive and thriving within the sound of the Liberty Bell in the City of Brotherly Love.

CHAPTER EIGHTEEN
In The Army Now

After the Japanese bombing of Pearl Harbor in 1941, The United States instituted the draft, in which all able-bodied men were required to sign up for possible induction into the armed services. Shortly after my graduation, I was classified 1A, which meant I would be among the first called to serve in the army, navy, army air corps (as it was called at that time) or marines. The army was the only service that utilized Black servicemen in positions other than heavy labor or kitchen duties. If you remember, Dorie Miller, who lost his life while manning a ship's machine guns and shooting down Japanese planes, left his duties in the mess hall to perform that heroic act.

Rather than take my chances, I volunteered in the army to take advantage of the specialty courses available.

I was very interested in a Signal Corps program that was administered at Philadelphia's Temple University. To be eligible you had to be in the top 100 group of college graduates who could master a study of math and electronics for a new radar program. If you passed the entrance test, wearing of the uniform was optional during the six week training period and the classes were held at night so as to not interfere with the University's day schedule. Temple was just a few blocks from my home, which was an additional advantage.

The entrance test was scheduled for 2PM, but the 98 White and 2 Black soldiers (including myself) had to report to the Temple campus at 9AM. We spent the waiting time shooting the breeze and finally the discussion got around to the race issue in the United States. The consensus among the White soldiers was that Black people had made great progress considering they were running around in the jungle a scant 1,000 years ago. Glancing over at us, they marveled that some of the former savages had even graduated from college. The highest mark possible on the entrance test was 150. The White soldiers continued to make their condescending racial remarks as we awaited the testing results at 4:30 PM.

An embarrassed hush descended on the Whites when it was announced that Charles Wright, the other African American, who later became a judge, scored 148 and I scored 147. None of the White "intelligentsia" scored higher than 138.

Another "Black stupidity" myth bit the dust.

Wright and I had the last laugh in that situation, but there was nothing funny about the humiliation suffered later by four of us in a Midwestern restaurant. That hurt has stayed with me for three quarters of a century.

CHAPTER NINETEEN
The Prisoners Win

After successfully completing radar training we were assigned to Camp Gruber, Oklahoma. Joining 98 more soldiers, including two more African Americans, we were ordered to escort 100 German prisoners-of-war to a prison at Camp Gruber. Taking great pains to check the handcuffs and other restraints of the Germans, we prepared for the long train ride from Philadelphia to Oklahoma. The Germans wore distinct, mustard colored prison garb with the word PRISONER emblazoned on the back.

The trip was uneventful until we stopped in Clairmont, Missouri, home of the late humorist Will Rogers, for a lunch break. We lined up the prisoners, still shackled, in front of a restaurant that had been commandeered ahead of time by the Army. The restaurant owner was rubbing his hands in glee at the large bill he anticipated charging the United States Government. Several White soldiers went ahead of the prisoners, the remainder marched alongside to prevent escape and we four Black soldiers brought up the rear.

When the restaurant owner saw the four of us, he went into a frenzy.

"No niggras, no niggras," he screamed

The Germans swiveled around, jeered our presence and began contemptuously shouting, "*schwarzen, schwarzen!*" "*Schwarzen*" means "niggers" and the prisoners, who pledged their allegiance to Adolph Hitler, had found four targets at which to spew their master race venom.

With equal contempt, the owner announced "if the niggras want to eat, they will have to go out (in the freezing February rain) to the back window where someone will make them sandwiches to take out."

Meanwhile, the German prisoners and the White soldiers sat in the warm, spacious dining room enjoying their meal. We Black soldiers were so angry that a bitter taste still surges to my throat when I remember that humiliating experience.

Fortunately, we did not have live ammunition in our weapons. I am not suggesting that the situation would have had a different conclusion, but one never knows, does one?

CHAPTER TWENTY
Outwitting The Colonel

We refused to go to the back window of the restaurant because that would have been a token of the acceptance of our humiliation. We walked, hungry and angry, back to the train and waited for the White soldiers and the prisoners.

You could have cut the guilt feelings of the returning soldiers with a machete as they got back on the train. The prisoners continued to snicker with contempt and that was the only sound heard during the remainder of a train ride that seemed to last forever.

When we finally disembarked at Camp Gruber, which I nicknamed Camp Gruesome, we were met with another unwelcome surprise. We had to wade through knee-deep mud to our barracks, only to find that sleeping quarters for Black soldiers were down in the valley, the reason for the mud. White soldiers slept in quarters up on the hill, high and dry.

Within six months, I was promoted to first sergeant, although I hadn't been in the army long enough to learn how to roll a back pack. The commanding officer of my unit, a captain, explained my rapid promotion by stating that "my service record revealed that I had a secure family background" and would "be least likely to panic in a battleground situation."

What the Captain really expected me to do was to report to him on the activities of my fellow Black soldiers. I decided to use his belief to our advantage.

I planted false reports with the Captain of a threatened revolt brewing in our group, without naming names. I promised to have more information of the threats by the following week.

My next report escalated the threat to the secret gathering of live ammunition in the barracks.

The captain alerted the base commander, a colonel, who sent his jeep to pick me up so he could confirm the "impending danger". Again, I asked for more time to gather specifics, still mentioning no names.

The following week I reported to the colonel that I had learned from reliable, though anonymous sources that the Black soldiers were upset about living in mud, poor food and no guest house, forcing them to travel 30 miles to Muskogee in order to enjoy a family visit.

In two months the food improved greatly, we were moved to dry living quarters and we were assigned a guest house on the base. I told the colonel that the threat of revolt had lessened and I assured him I would "keep an eye on things."

But the need for Black solidarity and creative use of my rank didn't end with that racial situation.

CHAPTER TWENTY-ONE
The Bombing Of Americans

The USO brought a show to the base for White soldiers only, because mixing of the races was illegal in Oklahoma. The Black soldiers really wanted to attend and they came to me for a solution. As the top non-commissioned officer, I had the keys to the rifle rack. The night of the show, I positioned 80 armed men behind rocks near the entrance of the building where the show was to be performed.

When the White soldiers showed up, I advised them orders had been issued barring their attendance at the show. They angrily rushed to military police (MP) headquarters to complain and returned with a jeep which contained four MPs.

The MPs asked who gave the order and I took the responsibility. As the MPs moved to take me into custody, I raised my hand and the loud clicks of 80 rifle bolts shattered the summer night.

Negotiations ensued and, finally, the Black troops were allowed to enter the building but they were not allowed to sit on the same side with Whites. That was the first unofficial act of integration at Camp Gruber. I was demoted one rank to tech sergeant for my role in the fight for equality. Later, I had a second brush with the MPs when I refused to sit in the back of a Muskogee public bus which was leased to the army. I received an official reprimand from the company commander, who was getting more than a bit weary of my militancy.

While stationed at Camp Gruber, I visited Greenwood, Oklahoma, an all-Black city that was the scene of a horrific invasion by Whites that killed over 300 African Americans and left more than 4,000 residents homeless.

Greenwood, which is near Tulsa, was known as "The Black Wall Street" in 1921. The city boasted 15 grocery stores, two movie theatres, several banks, 13 churches and numerous Black-owned businesses. The town had become arguably the most economically prosperous Black community in the United States.

Greenwood's prosperity drew the ire of a neighboring all-White community and led to a great deal of animosity.

Using the trumped-up, unfounded charge of a White woman raped by a Black man as revenge, the Whites burned 35 Greenwood city blocks to the ground, partially by dropping bombs from planes. It was the first bombing of Americans by Americans in United States history.

In addition, the Whites challenged the rebuilding efforts of Greenwood by refusing needed supplies. But Greenwood residents found a way to rebuild because, to paraphrase the words of the old African-American spiritual, "No man can-a hinder us."

I considered it a profound and historical opportunity to be able to speak with the survivors of that atrocity, which occurred only 21 years before my visit. It was yet another experience that would influence my future life's work. Then romance entered the picture.

CHAPTER TWENTY-TWO
Career-Ending Pain

There were lighter moments at Camp Gruber. In 1943, I married my fiancée, Oren Chester, of Philadelphia Pa., in the base chapel. The ceremony was complete with a crossed swords honor guard and a mini concert by the 20-voice 333d Field Artillery Battalion Choir, led by Eugene Wayman Jones. In addition to Jones' considerable musical skills, he won the silver medal for bravery under fire during the Battle of The Bulge in Europe. To add to his many accomplishments, Dr. Jones was later named the first Black professor of music at Temple University.

I brought my mother and my new mother-in-law to the post for the wedding ceremony and they were able to witness one of the most pleasant days of my army life.

Shortly after Oren and I moved into our Muskogee apartment, I began experiencing stomach pains. A thorough examination revealed a severe lesion on my duodenal that caused bleeding. While I was hospitalized, an event occurred that further confirmed the total societal permeation of Tarzanization mentioned in an earlier chapter. That event also taught me the critical importance of truthful knowledge of one's ancestral territory.

CHAPTER TWENTY-THREE
Red-Neck Wake-Up Call

In 1943, the hospital was the only facility not totally segregated in the armed forces. I imagine the cost of separate hospitals was too much even for the most rabid of racists. I was assigned to a ward where the patients were mostly White. During my 40-day stay there, a poor, semi-illiterate White soldier taught me why Black people are held in contempt by Whites, a lesson that shaped the rest of my life.

Our ward had a kitchen that had to be kept clean and orderly by the patients. As the top non-commissioned officer (first sergeant) in the ward, I had the task of assigning the "clean-up soldier" of the day. Not only was the cleaning duty nasty, but, because most of the patients were Southerners, taking orders from a Black non-com was equally unpleasant.

Private Jones, the soldier who taught me about White contempt, believed that any non-segregated activity was immoral, illegal, and blasphemous.

Finally, it was his turn to clean the kitchen. Not hearing any noise behind the adjoining kitchen door, I went to investigate.

Instead of cleaning up the day's mess, Private Jones was standing, arms folded and teeth clenched . When I asked him what the problem was, he replied angrily, " I just can't take no orders from a niggra."

I asked him. "Why not?"

He replied, "Because I am YOUR superior."

"Well," I reasoned, "There are three things that measure the superiority of a man: intelligence, knowledge and physical attributes. Now, what did you score on the army intelligence test?"

"I believe 95," he answered.

"I scored 147," I informed him. Now, how far have you gone in school?"

He brightened up. "I finished high school," he announced.

"I have a college degree," I announced again. His face fell.

"Finally," I snarled and made a menacing move toward him, "I can whip your ass, like, right now!"

"I guess you can," he answered, retreating several steps backward. "You're bigger and in better condition than I am."

"But there is a fourth thing," Private Jones proclaimed triumphantly.

"What is that?" I asked.

With a knowing grin, he replied, "I am your superior as a human being. I am descended from Europeans with their great civilizations and you are descended from apes who lived and thrived in the jungle."

"That is not true," I said aloud, but I thought to myself,

" He really, truly believes the lie and therein lies the real problem. I must come up with a deprogramming that will put that universal myth to rest."

Shifting back to the problem at hand, I said to Private Jones, "You are entitled to your beliefs, but that is no excuse to disobey an order from a superior officer. It is now court martial time."

The message was loud and clear. Private Jones filled a bucket with hot water, picked up a mop and started to clean up.

I am indebted to the Private Joneses of the world, be they in army barracks, halls of Congress, Boards of Education or Wall Street boardrooms, for confirming that *hatred and contempt of Black people is the programmed belief of the lack of African ancestral value. It is impossible to provide African ancestral value by only honoring African American achievement. This explains why eighty- five years of Black History month emphasis has done nothing to stem the increases of contempt, disrespect and disproportionate ills affecting Blacks in America and around the world.*

At that point in my life, I took a personal vow to study, teach, and amplify the importance of knowing and cherishing our African ancestral value. To Black people around the world, it can mean the difference between emotional freedom and intellectual death.

With army life behind me and with my new bride, I faced the necessity of obtaining a job in an industry engaged in the war effort.

CHAPTER TWENTY-FOUR
Return To "Brotherly Love"

After I was given an honorable discharge with a certificate of disability from the army in 1943, I moved back to Philadelphia, "The City of Brotherly Love" with my new bride. Oren and I moved in with my parents, who now lived in a slightly larger house.

As a condition of my discharge, I was required to work at least one year in a civilian job necessary to the war effort. I applied for a position with The Radio Corporation of America (RCA) in Camden , New Jersey. RCA qualified as a war effort company and promised career opportunities because of the electronics engineering certificate I earned from the army.

After an interview I was hired, but for an unusual reason. The human resources person explained there were "no colored people" in the department of which I was scheduled to be a part. She said they chose me, rather than a "dark colored person" to diminish "culture shock" in the elite department. I had been naïve enough to believe I would be hired because I was thoroughly qualified. Welcome back to the City of

Brotherly Love!

The job consisted of rolling thousands of coils contained in the systems of remote-controlled bombs. The system enabled the bomb to 'see' it's target before a strike.

I thought there had to be a way to solve the accuracy problem and reduce the number of people who painstakingly rolled the coils.

I worked at home in the basement and, over a three-week period, invented a system that rolled the coils automatically and accurately. My system, which RCA took credit for and ownership of, dramatically reduced the number of workers needed and saved the corporation thousands of dollars.

I expected a promotion, a large bonus and all the accoutrements. Instead, I was cited in a small corner of the department and presented the magnificent prize of a twenty-five dollar war bond.

Disappointed, I served the required year at RCA, cashed the war bond for eighteen dollars and seventy five cents and applied for my old job with Provident Home Industrial Mutual Life Insurance Company.

President Faison again welcomed me with open arms and I was given a debit (steady customers) which guaranteed a salary of fifty seven dollars a week! I was ecstatic and I hit the street, eager to add to my salary with commissions. In addition, my wife and I looked forward to a birth of a son.

CHAPTER TWENTY-FIVE
Protest in Philadelphia

Oren and I moved to our own apartment on the third floor over a store when our son, Edward, III, was born. I sold my Essex, bought a 1941 Dodge and made my insurance rounds burning thirty-five cents-a-gallon gasoline.

It was 1944 and returning Black servicemen were starting to question the America that sent servicemen overseas to fight injustice, yet practiced racial injustice at home.

As a glaring example of Philadelphia-style bias, Black people were barred from driving trolley cars, buses or trains. This injustice was perpetuated by the Transport Workers Union, which excluded Black people from membership. The Philadelphia Rapid Transportation Company (PRT) was able, like most all-white companies, to tell Black applicants, "Sure, we'll hire you. Just join the union." In order to join the all-White union, you had to be referred by another union member. The ploy was legal and worked for years until Black protesters, led by a fiery public schoolteacher named Goldie Watson, decided if Black people were good enough to ride, Black people were good enough to drive. My brother Calvin and I joined Mrs. Watson inpicket lines that were set up around City Hall, union headquarters and transportation depots. Fights broke out, and soon a mini-riot erupted, pitting White union members against Black picketers.

Selected White business windows were smashed in the melee, which caused a Chinese laundry owner, who lived across the street from me, to jump up and down and loudly proclaim, as an angry group approached his business, "Me nigger, me nigger." His instant change of ethnicity evoked waves of laughter and saved his glass window.

A court order ruled the transportation union's long-standing referral practice unconstitutional and ordered armed soldiers to ride with the first Black motormen and trainmen to shield them from White attacks. Philadelphia and the union later conspired to get Mrs. Watson fired from her school position with the help of the infamous Sen. Joe McCarthy and his witch hunt Communist hearings. With the help of motion pictures, the United States government was able to transform Russia, a World War II ally, into a hated and feared threat almost overnight and Sen. McCarthy was able to connect anyone affiliated with the civil rights struggle to the "Communist enemy."

Mrs. Watson was reinstated in her school position by winning her case before the United States Supreme Court, basing her winning argument on the powerful First Amendment of the Constitution which states: "Congress shall make no law… abridging… the right of the people peaceably to assemble."

Observing these incidents of injustice served to remind me that *every advancement of Black people in America is preceded by determined demand and a struggle.*

I was steered to my next big step by the words of my old college professor.

CHAPTER TWENTY-SIX
Buying My First Home

"We Black people must learn to make better use of our money." Professor George Singleton's Virginia State lecture was ringing in my ears as I prepared to make my first real estate purchase.

I sold my car, added the proceeds to my insurance commission income and placed a down payment on an apartment house with six units. My family lived in two units and rents from the other four covered the mortgage payment and utility bills.

I again called on my inventive skills to solve a problem caused by water overflowing a pan under our old-time ice box. I hooked up a system that would ring bells and flash lights before the water reached an overflow level.

My invention was the hit of the neighborhood and a friend loaned me money to have a patent registered.

But before I could reap any financial rewards, the electric refrigerator became popular. Another Black man, Frederick M. Jones, invented the electric refrigeration cooling system and my invention was obsolete.

With no car, I walked vast distances every day, in all kinds of weather, to service my insurance customers. The exercise not only kept me in physical shape, it helped me to save enough in auto expenses to buy a second apartment house in an even nicer North Philadelphia area.

Meanwhile, business had grown enough at Provident Home to allow the Company to move from the ramshackle building on Christian Street, to large, attractive headquarters at Broad and Fitzwater Streets. My brother, Calvin, was hired as an agent and made the move with us.

CHAPTER TWENTY-SEVEN
19 Years On Death Row

The year was 1948. Despite the steady barrage of injustices heaped on me, I was determined to win respect from the White community for Black folks by any means necessary.

Somewhere, earlier in my life, I was told that Black people were not respected because "they lacked education and financial stability." I had received an excellent education at Virginia State College and I was returning to the insurance business to do my part in building a million-dollar Black corporation.

In addition, I joined The League For Non-Violent Civil Disobedience Against Segregation In The Armed Forces headed by A. Phillip Randolph. Randolph also headed The Brotherhood Of Sleeping Car Porters Union, a labor group that fought for better working conditions for men who worked in the railroad system.

The League petitioned President Harry Truman for Executive Order 9981, which would outlaw segregation in the military forces. Opposition was fierce in both houses of Congress, the military establishment and in the White community. The usual racist arguments of mass morale problems and the doom of America as a world power prevailed.

In late 1948, Truman finally gave in to intense pressure from the League, and other civil rights groups and signed the Executive Order, which became effective in 1949. Senator McCarthy did not miss an opportunity to brand the League, the NAACP and other champions of racial justice as "Communist inspired."

I also joined a desperate effort to save seven young Black men from electrocution in the alleged rape of a 30-year Martinsville

Va. White woman. The youngest of the accused was only 13-years old!

The youths, called the Martinsville 7, testified the arresting officers brutally beat a "confession" from them. Court records show that the defense attorney stood idly by as the judge and jury convicted and sentenced to death the seven, despite the alleged victim's testimony that she was unable to identify any of the youths because it was dark in the room where the alleged rape took place.

During the trial, my brother, Calvin and I led a motorcade from Philadelphia to Richmond which surrounded the Virginia governor's mansion to protest the verdict, citing reasonable doubt and cruel and unusual punishment.

We had hoped the verdict would be reversed as it was in an earlier Scottsboro, Alabama "rape of White women" charge against nine innocent young Black men, labeled the Scottsboro 9.

Defense attorney Samuel Lebowitz, a brilliant, dedicated, Jewish lawyer, successfully exposed the lie of the two White prostitutes who, to save themselves from prostitution and vagrancy charges, were willing to see nine young Black men die in the electric chair. It took 19 years of expensive legal efforts before the last young defendant was exonerated.

My insurance business was accelerating and I was about to win a trip which had memorable consequences.

CHAPTER TWENTY-EIGHT
Millionaire Faces Sheriff

The year is 1951. My wife and I have two children and, as the number one sales producer at Provident Home, I was awarded a 21-day-all-expenses paid trip to Los Angeles, California, to attend a national insurance conference. My wife and son accompanied me and the top executives of the major Black insurance companies on a cross-country train excursion.

But, during that beautiful trip, I was jolted by an experience that shook the very foundation of my belief that economic stability of Black people would win honor and respect for the race.

Among our traveling companions was C.C. Spaulding, president of North Carolina Mutual Life Insurance Company and arguably the richest Black man in America. The train made a designated stop in Nevada and the conductor announced there would be a half-hour wait before our trip resumed. Mr. Spaulding, my son, now 6 and I decided to get off the train for an opportunity to "stretch our legs" during the waiting period.

We weren't on the ground 10 minutes before we were approached by a gun-toting, red-faced, beefy-looking man in cowboy boots and a wide-brimmed hat. Announcing he was the sheriff, he ordered the three of us back on the train, in no uncertain terms.

"Hold on," I protested, pointing to C.C. Spaulding, "Do you know to whom you are talking? This is the president of a multi-million dollar insurance company."

The sheriff waved his gun in the air and retorted, "If you-all don't get your black asses back on that train, he'll be the DEAD president of a multi-million dollar insurance company!"

I looked around for President Spaulding to back me up, but he had already raced back up the train steps as fast as his expensive-suited legs would carry him.

In the sheriff's racist mind, there were "rich niggras, poor niggras and dead niggras, your choice".

CHAPTER TWENTY-NINE
Money Takes Flight

Back on the train, C.C. Spaulding, my business idol, now with clay feet, apologized sheepishly for being so frightened as to run off and leave me and my son at the mercy of the irate sheriff.

Mr. Spaulding's personal wealth and his building of a $120 million dollar business had accomplished financial heights and stability that I was told would win the respect and honor of Black people from White people. "When money talks, racism walks" was the balloon floated over the heads of oppressed African Americans.

But this theory came crashing down in the face-off between Mr. Spaulding's financial heights and the threat of the sheriff's six-shooter.

Several years before this incident, I had begun wondering what the *real* problem was behind the disproportionate ills suffered by Black people in America. It seemed that many of the problems we suffered were merely *manifestations of the real problem and the solutions we sought were just veils of illusions.*

Negro History Weeks came and went and we learned about great scientists like Dr. George Washington Carver, brave military men like Gen. Benjamin O. Davis, Jr., great entertainers like Lena Horne, pioneers in medicine like Dr. Daniel Hale Williams and the list seemed endless.

Despite our History Week progress, my elementary school teachers told me the lack of education was our problem. When the German prisoners-of war were ushered into the Oklahoma dining room, we four Black soldiers who were barred were in graduate school. So much for lack of education, a veil of illusion.

Black people were told that a lack of jobs kept us from being respected. But from 1619 until 1865 we were fully employed from childhood until death and not an iota of respect or honor came our way.

So much for job scarcity, another veil of illusion.

The question began to creep into my mind: *Is Negro History Week yet another veil, hiding the real problem?*

Are we on the right railroad, but the wrong track?

I began to dip into my memory stream.

CHAPTER THIRTY
Motion Picture Power

During the next few years, my hospital conversation with Private Jones kept bouncing around in my head.

He believed the lie that the ancestors of Black people were savages, so the true history of African Americans was the right railroad. On the other hand, I was concerned that highlighting the accomplishments of a few people born *after* our captivity was the wrong track.

But because of the power of such movies as "Tarzan", "Birth of A Nation," "Gone With The Wind" and "Amos and Andy," I was concerned with the difficulty of getting America on the right track of recognizing the Songhai people as the true ancestors of African Americans.

The Songhai Empire, which was located below the Sahara desert in an area larger than the Europe, reached its zenith less than 500 years ago. The Empire boasted world-class universities, beautiful homes, tree-lined streets, fabulous shops, a gold standard, a judicial system and kings and queens.

But I was so involved with Provident Home's steady financial progress and my predicted goal of the company becoming a million dollar business, the solution of the wrong or right track to solve the real problem of our people would have to wait.

CHAPTER THIRTY-ONE
Auction Blocks Revisited

Provident Home Life Insurance Company was part of an organization of sixty-seven Black-owned life insurance companies throughout the United States. The organization, The National Insurance Association (NIA), developed two-week summer management courses to which they sent their executives. I was appointed a member of the faculty by the NIA to teach a course at these seminars, which were held at various Black universities.

In 1968, I had a life-changing experience during a session at Dillard University, in New Orleans.

I took my class on a walking tour down Bourbon Street in the Old French Quarter. A stone's throw from the Mississippi River, of "Old Man River" fame were little 4x4x4 cages in which the more militant of our enslaved fathers were placed. There they were kept, in cramped agony, day after day. They were supplied with little water or food, barely enough to sustain life, until their White captors thought their spirit was sufficiently broken. Farther on down Bourbon Street, where the street curves, was preserved an auction block from which our ancestors were sold. I pointed out to my class that the grooves on the auction block were made by the dragging of the chains of our fathers and mothers. I told them that among the captives were, doctors, lawyers, college professors, governors of provinces and mayors of cities.

Suddenly, the sound of the Mississippi lapping on that stony beach faded from my ears, as did the murmurs of my class.

And there, appearing before me on the auction block, was a moving, quietly-speaking crowd of people, dressed in colorful, but tattered elegance. They wore robes of nobility with head wraps (gelas) of the same material and finely-wrought leather shoes.

Suddenly, a loud, piercing voice from the crowd in my vision exhorted, *"Edward, tell them who we are!"*

Then, as suddenly as the vision appeared, it faded. I was again aware of the sound of The Mississippi River and the mur-muring of my students.

"Why me?" I wondered, as I replayed the urgency of the voice again and again in my head.

That afternoon, I addressed the graduating NIA class. After my speech, several people commented that there seemed to be lights dancing around my head as I spoke. I tried to credit the "lights" to an illusion created by the glare of the summer sun com-ing into the auditorium through the windows. But, from that day on, I became dedicated to the direction of the voice in my vision.

CHAPTER THIRTY-TWO
Angry Neighbors

I continued to do well at Provident Home and in 1951, I wanted to move my family from our North Philadelphia apartment to a beautiful single-family home in West Philadelphia. But when we contacted the real estate agent for the home my wife and I had fallen in love with, we were told the home owner would not sell to Black people.

Using African ingenuity, I made a successful bid on the house by having a White friend pose as a buyer with my Black agent. But then I found it was really the neighbors who had brought pressure on the realtor not to sell to African Americans. In fact, the leader of the largely-Irish area was a Catholic priest who, on behalf of the all-White residents, offered the seller one thousand dollars not to sell to me.

The seller, who was German-American, decided to get back at the Irish, who, earlier, accused him of being a "Nazi sympathizer." "I'll punish them by selling to you," he told me, not realizing that his revenge was an insult of the highest degree to me. I was pleased to be able to buy the home, but it took tremendous restraint on my part to keep from cussing him out in a most non-professional way.

I started to receive threats and insults even before I could move into my new home. My home was in the middle of the block and as a sign of disrespect, White families up and down the block deliberately turned their porch furniture away from my home's location. Whites glared at us with obvious hostility if we chanced to glance their way.

Finally, I decided enough was enough. No more "Mr. Nice Negro".

I wrapped a broom in brown paper so it looked like a rifle in its case, put on my army uniform and sat on my porch with my "rifle" across my knees. Waving my "rifle" menacingly, I announced in a booming voice, "I was a sharpshooter in the army and I volunteered to fight for YOUR freedom. Now it's time to fight for mine. Anyone who puts a foot on my pavement will get a bullet between the eyes!"

I couldn't hide the smile on my face for weeks as I saw White folks timidly stepping into the street before warily approaching my house.

Now comfortably settled in the new home, I pondered the next career move.

CHAPTER THIRTY-THREE
Chimpanzee Visits Law School

The increasing positive financial position and the mounting financial complexities at Provident Home, plus, the increasing need for protection of Black people struggling against the injustice of segregation, propelled me toward getting a legal degree.

I took and passed easily the entrance exam for law school and entered the evening class at Temple University Law School in September, 1953.

Incidentally, my admission to law school occurred eight months before the landmark Supreme Court decision which declared unconstitutional state laws establishing separate schools. The unanimous decision was believed to pave the way for integration and the civil rights movement.

During my four years of law school, Provident Home reached the million-dollars-in-assets mark and I was appointed manager of the Philadelphia district, the company's largest.

I was still an agent on the street while attending law school. After having supper with my family and playing with my children, for I headed to classes until 10:30 each weekday night. After school, my home study period lasted until about 3AM.

My study technique was based on a picture being worth a thousand words. During class, I took copious notes on the left half of my notebook page. At night, along with corresponding textbook information, I translated the notebook notes into pictures, which I drew on the right hand half of my notebook. Just before test time, I studied the pictures and successfully passed the exams.

From my second year to graduation, I was the only Black person in class. My fellow students took offense at the constitutional law professor's habit of referring to me as "the colored fellow." I told them "it doesn't matter what *you people* call me." Puzzled by my answer, one of them, an Italian, asked, "Suppose we call you a nigger?"

I replied, "As you know, chimpanzees are becoming more able to communicate by using a computer.

Suppose a chimp called you a '*dago*'. Would you get angry?"

"No," the Italian replied.

"Why not?" I asked.

"The chimp is an animal and doesn't know any better," he replied.

I shot back, "That's exactly what I would think of *you.*"

Another law school incident dealt with one of the favorite topics of White people: the comparison of Black people and apes.

One evening, as I entered a long hallway at school, I saw a large group of my fellow students gathered around a bulletin board. They noticed my approach and tried, in vain, to suppress their laughter. I saw that they were looking at five or six pictures of apes in various comic poses. Expecting a personal attack, my ego antennae went up instantly. I asked the group what was so funny.

Laughingly, they replied, " Doesn't this ape look amazingly like Jackson (a richly pigmented former fellow student)?

After closely studying the picture, I answered, "Since we will be lawyers soon, we should seek to look at things analytically. First, what kind of hair does this ape in the picture have?"

They looked closely at the ape and answered, "Straight."

"That's correct," I agreed , "Just like yours," and I pointed directly at Jim, a White Anglo Saxon Protestant a fellow student, who was laughing the hardest.

The sound of condescending ridicule began to diminish as I asked the group to examine the ape's profuse body hair, his close-set eyes, his thin lips, his flat buttock muscle, and his large, wiggling ears, all of which are distinct Caucasian and chimpanzee characteristics, not African features.

By this time, Jim was desperate, sweating profusely and not happy at all. The rest of the White students shared Jim's discomfort.

Then Jim received an epiphany.

"Hold it, hold it Ed. You haven't mentioned the BIG thing!"

"What's the BIG thing?" I asked innocently.

"His COLOR," Jim exclaimed victoriously. "The ape is black, just like you people." The crowd, which had grown considerably, cheered in agreement.

"Oh no," I replied. "You're just looking at the ape's hair. The ape's skin looks just like yours." I gestured with my hands to include all the White folks in the hallway. The crowd's objection was loud, incredulous and disbelieving.

"I'll tell you what," I continued in response to the vocal disapproval, "I'm not a betting man, but I will prove my point, *to Jim's satisfaction. Who will match me?"* I asked, placing one hundred dollars in Jim's hand. They quickly collected another hundred dollars, gave it to Jim and awaited my proof.

I called the Philadelphia zoo and asked for the supervisor of the house where apes and higher anthropoids are kept. When he came to the phone, I disguised my voice by holding my nose and speaking in a "White" nasal tone.

"This is Temple University," I announced. "We are having a moot court discussion involving the chimpanzee. What is the skin color of the chimpanzee and other higher anthropoids?"

"Aren't you the same fellow who called two weeks ago asking the same question?" he asked.

"Please, just answer the question" I replied.

The supervisor yelled so loud, everyone standing close heard his reply: "The same color it was two weeks ago. *The skin is a pinkish white.* I asked him to repeat his answer and pressed the telephone receiver against Jim's ear. Jim was in shock as I removed two hundred dollars from his pinkish white hands.

Even today that comparison myth is alive and well, but after the zoo experience, discussions of race went smoothly in the evening Temple University Law School class of 1957.

IN LIVING COLOR: This photo of a young chimpanzee
helped Dr. Robinson win a discussion with students
at Temple University Law School.

CHAPTER THIRTY-FOUR
No Function, No Value

There was one thing I could not understand about White people until later in my life.

Socially, every thing would be fine if we were playing soccer, running track, studying in the library, or meeting in a school committee. But, the same day, if I met the same White people they would turn away and not speak if I met them away from the soccer field, the track, the library or the school committee meeting .

When I discussed this phenomenon with friends and relatives, we decided this experience was *functional acceptance* — in other words, their acceptance of you only while in a particular function in which you both operate.

Later, I learned that it is more than just function by itself — it's that you have *value to them in that function*.

That functional value is part of a larger value called *extrinsic* value.

An understanding of *intrinsic* and *extrinsic* value can be learned from the real-life experience of pro basketball great Bill Russell, who was a star with the Boston Celtics during the 1960's. White and Black basketball lovers shook the rafters of Boston Garden with their cheers as Russell, a member of the Basketball Hall of Fame, performed outstanding feats on both offense and defense. When he played his last game, gifts and accolades of praise followed the retirement of his jersey number during the half-time ceremony.

A frightening turn of events followed just a few days after the retirement celebration. Police had to be called to protect Russell from an angry White mob, who tried to prevent him from moving into a beautiful home he had purchased in "their" neighborhood.

Russell was accepted as a basketball star because he *functionally gave great value to the White-owned Boston Celtic team. His value was extrinsic. But the mobs still looked down upon him and did not want him living near them because he lacked intrinsic or ancestral value in their eyes.*

I would learn much more about *extrinsic* and *intrinsic* value during the next big chapter in my life—the Roaring Sixties.

CHAPTER THIRTY-FIVE
Freedom Now!

The 60's roared in following the dynamite combination of the student sit-ins in the southern part of the country, the bravery of Mrs. Rosa Parks and the eloquence of Rev. Dr. Martin Luther King, Jr.

We Philadelphians caught the "Freedom Now" fever too. We formed the Black People's Unity movement (BPUM), led by Black activists Walter Palmer, Mattie Humphrey, Fred Bonaparte, Calvin Robinson and myself. Father Paul Washington lent BPUM a permanent meeting place at his huge Church of the Advocate, located in North Philadelphia.

What had initially excited us was the experiment of John Churchville, who, some years before, had taken a large group of pre-school Black children and taught them about the grandeurs of 15th and 16th Centuries Africa.

He surrounded his store-front "school" with large pictures of the Great Pyramids, the pictures of Black kings and queens of ancient Egypt (Kemet) and the empire of Songhai.

The children at Churchville's "school" learned reading and writing and were far ahead of their public school in the first and second grades.

The children began losing their initial enthusiasm, academic proficiency and beautiful behavior when entering third grade.

Searching for a cause, we observed there were no positive pictures of African grandeur and royalty on display in public schools.

Instead, Abe Lincoln, George Washington and various "Dick and Jane" images were prominently featured.

In addition, most of the public schools in North Philadelphia bore the names of White people, further enhancing the *intrinsic value* of Caucasian alignment.

BPUM began separating into various programs, called ministries. The political ministry had as its goal attacks on injustices that occur in the Black community. It also summoned various political figures into meetings to "keep their feet to the fire" on issues benefiting the Black community. This ministry was headed by the powerful Walter Palmer, who went on to get a law degree and founded a charter school to better follow his passion.

BPUM formed a theatrical ministry to gather young people who loved to act and wanted to learn the behind-the- scenes techniques involved in presenting meaningful stage productions. This ministry evolved into Freedom Theatre, a production company that went on to earn fame and stature across America.

BPUM also formed the Community Schools Ministry, led by my brother, Calvin and me. This ministry started as a gathering place for teachers and neighbors to discuss more productive methods of educating Black children. During these meetings I was fortunate to meet Dr. Walter Lomax and his beautiful wife, Beverly. The Lomaxes invited Calvin and me to their home on numerous occasions and we were introduced to many of their friends and neighbors, creating close relationships that persist to this day.

In addition, Dr. Lomax became a dedicated philanthropist, aiding scores of organizations involved in the Black struggle.

BPUM also created a Mass Communications Ministry, which taught how the press, TV and movies consistently devalued the intrinsic worth of Black people with language, image and placement. Fred Bonaparte, who was a newspaper editor at the time, guided this effort.

As BPUM grew larger and its impact more meaningful, meetings began to center around what was so evident in the Community Schools Ministry. There was an essential need for corrective African history to be taught to *everyone*, especially in the public schools. The academic playing field could never be leveled with European history taught at every turn and corrective African his-

tory ignored completely. I searched for an opportunity to demon-
strate to Board of Education officials how achievement scores
for Black children soared when they were taught at John Churchville's store-front "freedom" school. I was hoping for something
to happen which could prove conclusively the academic value of
African history.

CHAPTER THIRTY-SIX
The Mathematics Experiment

The opportunity arose in the mid-Sixties when public school teachers went out on strike for several weeks. I asked School Superintendent, Dr. Mark Shedd, for 100 Black students who scored the lowest marks in math during the school term. He received permission from the parents of 114 children and had them bussed to BPUM classes at the Church of The Advocate in North Philadelphia.

Dr. Shedd and I agreed that the children would be divided into a control group and an experimental group, each being taught how to do word problems, the most difficult math for Black children.

I enlisted the assistance of Dr. Clarence Harris, a great math teacher and General Electric engineer, who invented the panels which protected space craft from heat destruction when entering the atmosphere. Dr. Harris taught the control group of 57 students how to solve word problems six hours a day, from Monday to Friday.

I took the experimental group of 57. On Monday, Tuesday and half-a-day Wednesday, I taught them they were the descendants of Black people who built the Great Pyramid, the most magnificent structure in the world. I taught them that the Black-skinned Astronomer Priestesses of Egypt gave the world geometry, trigonometry and calculus. I also taught them that it was Ahmos, a Black Egyptian, who created algebra 3700 years ago and his book can be found today in the British Museum in London, England.

I taught the students that Black people only make up 7% of the world's population, yet with 80% of the gold medals in Olympic track and field events. I showed them a picture of a 9,000-year-old vase which had the words "fraction one-half" inscribed on it in the ancient Egyptian language. The children were able to witness African reading, writing and mathematics *nine millennia* ago. On the other hand, the first European book, "The Iliad" was written by Homer only 2,800 years ago. And I taught them many other things.

That Friday we gave the same mathematics test in word problems to all 114 hitherto "poor" math students.

All of the students passed, but the children who studied African history first and math only two-and-a-half days, scored significantly higher than the control group, which studied math the full four-and-a-half days. The test was administered and scored by the Curriculum Department of the Philadelphia School District, which reported the results to Dr. Shedd.

AHMOSE, A Black African ancient Egyptian scribe, created algebra 3700 years ago. His papyrus, discovered in his tomb in the mid-nineteenth century, was donated to a British museum. The particular problem on this page, is solved by means of an unknown quantity. This is the earliest existence of algebraic procedure.

CHAPTER THIRTY-SEVEN
Violence In The Streets

Astonished by the results, the Superintendent decided to institute the teaching of African and African American history from kindergarten through twelfth grade.

Now we had proof of how children thrive educationally and emotionally when they learn of the greatness of their ancestral home.

BPUM leaders, fired up with this knowledge, planned a protest march on School District Headquarters November 17, 1967. Five thousand students from all over the city amassed at the 21st and Parkway building pleading for their African history to be taught.

At the same time, Dr. Shedd had invited several of the BPUM leaders into the School District boardroom.

The brutality seen through School District windows, of student marchers beaten by police, will forever be a horrific blot on Pennsylvania history.

When police were ordered by the police chief to "get them off the streets," some of us at the meeting couldn't contain ourselves as the children were attacked. We ran outside and I tried, to no avail, grabbing the club of a huge cop who was beating David P. Richardson Jr., my 19-year-old nephew. David, three years later, was elected Pennsylvania's youngest state legislator ever.

David had prostrated himself over a 13-year old girl to absorb the blows meant for her. Fortunately, David had a huge Afro which absorbed the blows and saved him from a skull fracture or worse. He was hand-cuffed behind his back and arrested with many other students.

Assault charges against the students were dropped in court when defense lawyers, led by the late Cecil B. Moore, proved the students were peaceably marching around the building at the time of the police attack. When Moore asked a testifying police-man how David could have committed an assault with his hands cuffed behind his back, the cop could only stammer and shuffle in confusion.

To add insult to injury, all the police officers, including the chief, were cleared of brutality. The testimonies of many witnesses to the contrary, were ignored.

But, the question remained: *How could we implement the adding of African history to the school curriculum?*

The answer seemed obvious. There had to be top-level administration promotion.

In the Sixties, the School Board hired White contractors to begin the building of a school at 32nd Street and Ridge Ave., an all-Black neighborhood. BPUM observed that there were no Black subcontractors on the job and vowed to halt construction on the site until Black subcontractors were hired.

Two BPUM members and I stopped all work by lying in front of a contractor's bulldozer all night. Then we were relieved by other BPUM members on the day shift.

The contractor gave in, sent Black subcontractors to the job site and the work continued.

CHAPTER THIRTY-EIGHT
The Personality Parade

Dr. Shedd asked the leaders of BPUM to form a committee to interact with the School Board to get African History taught. We first appointed educators, mainly principals of Black schools to the committee. We then added outstanding community activists who were members of BPUM. Next, I added two White first-year high school students to find out if a knowledge of African history would change any negative attitudes they had about Black people.

Dr. Shedd appointed school administrator Ms. Constance Clayton, who later became school superintendent, to the group, which was formally named "The Ad Hoc Administration Committee For the Infusion of African and African American Heritage Into the Curricula."

The meetings were held at least once a week for four years and William Spang and Ina Durkov, the White students, were extraordinarily bright and attentive.

The first issue tackled was the amount of time to be spent studying *African history* as compared with *African American history*.

Dr. Edith Ingram, principal of an elementary school, reported she had been teaching *African American* history to every child in every class, every week (not just in February), but *no African history*. Since this had been her practice for many years, we were anxious to learn the impact on the students. Dr. Shedd commissioned a research team to discover if the study of *only* African American history had a positive affect on student achievement. She was heart-broken to learn the learning skills and behavior of her students were *the same* as students who only observed Black History Week once a year.

I suspected strongly that only the study of African history would make a positive, measurable difference.

I was told by a Jewish scholar that synagogue schools teach their children the history of *only* ancient Israel, not Jewish American history. The children do not even learn the story of Haym Solomon, who financed the American revolutionary War.

I sought answers to three other observations: *Why were Jewish scholars consistently outstanding graduates from Philadelphia's famed Central High School (from which I graduated)?*

Although Jewish people make up only two percent of America's population, why are 46% of the top American universities headed by Jewish presidents?

Finally, why is the fratricide (brother killing brother) rate among Jews practically negligible?

Intriguing answers came from a book entitled *The Territorial Imperative,* written by Robert Ardrey.

The book proves that *only when humans are taught to love and honor their ancestral land and its outstanding ancestors, can they reach the height of their intelligence and creative potential.* This practice of teaching and learning starts with Jewish children at birth.

I felt the challenge to us, as descendants of world-respected cultural excellence, was as clear as the pristine waters of an African mountain stream.

We needed an African history textbook and guess who would have to write it?

CHAPTER THIRTY-NINE
Fear Of The Truth

When the Committee asked me to orchestrate the writing of the African infusion history book, I enlisted the assistance of the brilliant scholar Dr. John Henrik Clarke, who planned the outline. We completed the writing of the book entitled "The World of Africans and Afro-Americans," which was copyrighted by the School District of Philadelphia in 1969.

Although the book was heralded as a stunning success, it was published as a separate book and not included within the chapters of textbooks used in school study.

I personally rode the trucks that delivered thirteen thousand copies of "The World of Africans and Afro-Americans" throughout the school system. However, I was terribly disappointed to find out the books were never used. Many teachers said they were not used because the information in the books was not included in classroom textbooks. Nearly thirty years later, a huge number of unused "The World of Africans and Afro- Americans" books were found stacked in classroom closets.

In addition to writing the book, the Ad Hoc Committee asked me to write an "African and African-American History" curriculum for a ten-week in-service course for teachers. I was head of the 15-member faculty of community activists who taught the course to two thousand teachers at many Philadelphia Jr. and Sr. High schools. I taught my class, which my present wife, Harriette, attended, at Strawberry Mansion Jr. High School in North Philadelphia.

An interesting thing occurred during the filming of the course, which was shown throughout the school district.

I had insisted that the story of the chimpanzee that I told in law school be filmed, directed by the late Matt Robinson, of "Sesame Street" and "Bill Cosby Show" fame.

In the film, the narrator pointed to the various characteristics of the chimpanzee, including the narrow nose, the close-set eyes and the undeveloped (flat) buttock muscle.

However, when the narrator raised a little flap of hair on the chest of the stuffed chimpanzee, exposing a white skin, the School Board Committee "went bananas."

When the Ad Hoc Committee asked for an explanation, the Administration argued that the showing of the chimpanzee's white skin color would be "embarrassing" to White students. Our counter argument that Black students had suffered incorrect comparison to the chimpanzee's skin color for decades fell on deaf ears and the Ad Hoc Committee was forced to remove the white skin scenes from the film.

However, the Ad Hoc Committee created the Department of African and African American History, which functioned for the next thirty-five years.

The committee had labored well. What would spin off in the exit interviews?

CHAPTER FORTY
"Intelligent Apes"

The exit interviews that were given members of the Committee at it's dissolution were recorded and became part of the formal minutes.

One of the most informational interviews was that of the two White students. When asked what they thought of African Americans after four years of learning of their history, they both replied, "We still think that Black people are highly intelligent apes."

That statement "blew the minds" of the Ad Hoc Committee members. They looked at me for an answer to this question: *"If all the knowledge we poured into their minds, week after week in the last four years, didn't change their negative attitudes of Black people, what will?*

I explained that the information which did not change the attitude of White students *would* have a positive effect on Black students because it would *awaken their territorial imperative.*

There are two powerful impediments to the acceptance of positive Black information by White people. *One is the White genetic rejection by their amygdala (a walnut-sized portion of the brain that triggers fear and alarm when it sees someone of a different race) of Black people.*

The other is the constant bombardment of anti-African sentiment by the communications media. Neither can be overcome from the four years of information the White students had learned.

Instead, there has to be the subliminal impact of motion picture drama. The drama must be a story line which includes at least some of the six ingredients of emotion: love, sex, violence, suspense, mystique and closure. These ingredients produce a sword that penetrates the subconscious and changes attitudes.

Society's attitude toward Black people can be affected positively by subliminally showing the beauty, grandeur and sophistication of the 16th and 17th Centuries' culture of the West African and Egyptian (Kemet) ancestors of present-day African-Americans.

Meanwhile, Dr. Shedd made plans to infuse African and African American history into the public school curriculum. When news of his decision reached the mayor, the word was passed that Dr. Shedd's job was on the line if he followed through with his program.

At the beginning of the next term, the superintendent began instituting the reprinting of history books to include corrective African history.

He was fired immediately.

I failed in my efforts to persuade subsequent superintendents to include in the texts of *all first-to-eighth-grade children* the greatness of the West African (Songhai) culture of the ancestors of African Americans. The superintendents ignored me, were intimidated, or hired me and *they* were terminated. I discovered other historians like me had similar experiences.

We came to the conclusion that there had to be *A CONSPIRACY TO PREVENT BLACK CHILDREN FROM HAVING A LEVEL PLAYING FIELD IN ACADEMIA FOR FEAR THEY WOULD DOMINATE AS BLACKS DO IN OTHER LEVEL FIELDS.*

CHAPTER FORTY-ONE
History Of The Spirituals

Meanwhile, I spoke all over the city and state on behalf of BPUM's Community Schools Ministry. My talks were a consistent effort to alert students, teachers and administrators to the importance of including corrective African History in school curriculums.

As part of my talks, I added the history of "spirituals", which I called "signal songs". I told my audiences how our ancestors outsmarted the captors by using the drum to pass along escape instructions from plantation to plantation. When the drums were outlawed, our fathers and mothers used our "spirituals" to communicate messages that could mean the difference between life and death.

For example, the song "Wade In The Water" was used to warn escaping captives to run in the water so their scent would be more difficult to follow by tracking bloodhounds.

I sang the songs, accompanied by my long-time friend and pianist, Fred Bonaparte.

One morning, Fred taped my presentation at William Penn High School, an all-girls school in North Philadelphia. A few years later, after hearing me speak, Barry Hampe, the director of the Annenberg School of Communications at the University of Pennsylvania, insisted that one of my talks, complete with music, should be recorded. Hampe, a White Georgian, had burst into tears after hearing the presentation.

The Annenberg School made the William Penn High tape into an album we called "Black Rhapsody".

We were delighted when the William Penn principal wrote that the impact of "Black Rhapsody" so profoundly affected the students, that the largest percentage of the graduating class in the school's history went on to college.

"Black Rhapsody" contained the memorable story of the little eagle who was told he was just a dark chicken, but discovered he was descended from kings of the sky.

By a conservative estimate, "Black Rhapsody" was presented to at least three thousand audiences in schools, churches and corporations over the next twenty years.

I must pause to say that Fred Bonaparte has been not only my accompanist, but a loyal friend of many years.

In 1968, I underwent a serious operation and during the period after the surgery, I floated in and out of consciousness over many hours. I remember to this day his constant healing presence each time I opened my eyes, day and evening.

Fred is serving today as my writing helper, drawing upon his skills honed as city editor of the Philadelphia Tribune during the sixties and seventeen years as advertising representative and manager with Philadelphia's Evening and Sunday Bulletin.

CHAPTER FORTY-TWO
The Songhai People

The other part of BPUM's School's Ministry was the gathering of a huge amount of historical data needed for our teaching and community engagements.

Calvin, my brother, Redman Battle, a friend and I wrote "The Journey Of The Songhai People" based on that accumulated data and published in 1988. The book received the accolades of many people, including Dr. Molefi Asante, who said it was "the greatest foundational book in African History known to him."

"The Journey" as it is known in shorthand, is used as a basic book which three thousand students had to study to qualify for a free trip to Africa.

The book is so popular because it lays bare the truths of the West African ancestors of African-Americans and the Diaspora. "The Journey" documents our fathers and mothers were of world-class literacy, not illiterate savages. "The Journey" informs that our fathers and mothers lived in beautiful homes, made of polished stones, on tree-lined avenues, not huts made of scrap wood. "The Journey" discloses that Songhai supplied 80% of the world's gold for several centuries. "The Journey" reveals that Homer said in his *Iliad* over 2800 years ago, *"the very gods of Greece travel to Africa to sup with Africa's faultless people."*

CHAPTER FORTY-THREE
Catholic University Shock

Despite an activity-filled schedule during the Sixties and Seventies, I managed to squeeze several teaching assignments into my busy work week.

I was appointed a member of the history faculty at Cabrini University, a predominately White , upper income, all-girls, Catholic institution just outside of Philadelphia.

I got off to a really good offensive start by teaching my class of thirty, which included one Black student, of the spectacular history of Songhai and ancient Egypt (Kemet). I could sense the suppressed giggles and whispers as I expanded on the royal background of present-day African-Americans.

In the middle of my lecture, I played the tape of a talk radio show. The rasping voice of an Irish woman stopped the giggles and immediately caught the attention of my students.

In a voice, dripping with disgust, the woman complained, "They're dirty. It's no wonder we don't want to be around them. And they're stupid. It's a waste of money to build schools for them, because they're too stupid to learn!"

I stopped the tape.

"There's more," I explained. "but, before we go any further, about whom is she speaking?"

The giggles were no longer suppressed and a number of hands shot up.

The students tried to be polite, but the answers were unanimous. "She's speaking about "you people."

Some said "negroes" or "colored people."

"Is there agreement on that answer? I asked, knowing there was. All hands went up in assent, including the Black girl's.

I pushed "play" and the woman's voice on the tape continued in an angry shriek. "And we Protestants of Ireland have to unite in the fight against those dirty Catholics!"

The room was so silent, you could have heard a gnat alighting on a marshmallow.

Finally, as the students struggled to recover from their shock, I explained: "The basic point I will try to get home to you this term is, *a brainwash is a terrible thing!"*

The young ladies showed me the utmost, most carefully crafted respect for the remainder of the term.

CHAPTER FORTY-FOUR
Classroom Surprise

Later, I accepted a position on the faculty of the Bucks County Community College, another upper income school in the suburbs of Philadelphia.

The evening class consisted of about thirty adults, all White (or so I thought).

My curriculum was more in depth about physical appearance than it was at Cabrini College because I had finessed the Bucks County adults into accepting the hard facts of the chimpanzee's appearance.

During the first night in class, I asked the students to submit, anonymously, any question they had on race and I would attempt an answer during the course of the term.

As expected, one of the early questions asked was: "Isn't it true that the real reason you people are looked down upon is because you haven't evolved much past the ape?"

When I had a student read that question aloud, the efforts of the other students to keep the smiles off their faces put a smile on mine.

There is no greater pleasure than to see the smiles of amused contempt slowly fade as the hard facts are hammered home. The red faces and lowered eyes all appeared just as they did in law school many years previously (see pages 80-81).

Then I continued, answering the other questions while weaving in the spectacular facts of our fathers and mothers not only contributing to civilization, but _creating civilization._

I thought it was an all-White class, but a few weeks before the end of the term, I invited the class to the beautiful East Mount Airy home of one of my Black friends for drinks. One of my students, Linda McPherson, the whitest-appearing person in the class with her flowing blonde hair, asked to see me privately.

As we entered an adjoining room, Linda took out her wallet and showed me the picture of a stately, elderly Black lady.

Linda said, in a raised, intense voice, "That's my grandmother. I'm Black and I can't wait to tell these (expletives) in the next room how I got this scar on my head." She parted her hair and showed me a nasty, jagged, healed wound.

"My family lived in a small suburb of Los Angeles. When the Whites found out we were Black, they chased us out of town, throwing bricks. One of the bricks hit me in the head. I was just a teenager."

I took her hands in mine and she agreed to wait before disclosing her experience to anyone.

At the beginning of the next class session I said, "I thought this class was all-White. I have since discovered that a person living among you is Black. At the proper time, that person will be revealed to you".

You would have thought I had announced the planting of a time bomb in one of the vending machines! My phone rang off the hook in the week before our last class session.

"Dr. Robinson," the callers explained. "Not that race is important, but everybody is blaming everyone else. We're going crazy out here!"

I had a standard response to the frantic callers. "If you're saying color and race don't matter, why are you using words like 'blame'?"

There was standing room only in my last class, despite the extra chairs that were brought in. Anticipation filled the room and I doubt if anyone heard my final lecture.

Finally, I said, "Will the person who wishes to reveal his or her Blackness come to the front of the room? Now is the time".

There was a very long silence. Then slowly, ever so slowly, Linda stood up to a hundred gasps of disbelief.

She told the class she came among them as a Vista worker. She berated them for the hypocrisy they demonstrated in their racist comments about Black people.

She pointed fingers and named names in the class.

She ended by saying she would probably be run out of Bucks County and have bricks thrown at her as the "racists like you" did in Los Angeles. She then parted her hair and showed the class the ugly scar.

A white student stood and announced he would like to escort her to a little affair I was hosting to celebrate the end of the semester.

Her refusal was courteous but final.

"No thank you", she replied. "I have discovered that my West African ancestors were royalty. I don't need any small favors".

THIS IS AN IMAGE of fifteen century Timbuktu, home of Songhaians. Note the three-story homes made of polished stone sitting on a tree-lined avenue. The University of Sankore is in the background. Here, beginning in 2001, tens of thousands of trunks were dug up. The trunks, buried 400 years earlier, contained hundreds of thousands of books.

PICTURED ARE SOME of the hundreds of thousands of books retrieved from tens of thousands of trunks buried by ancestors of African Americans (and Diasporans) 400 years ago. This picture appeared in the December, 2006, Smithsonian Magazine. The purpose of the gigantic burials was to give their descendants irrefutable proof of the world-class literacy of their West African ancestors.

CHAPTER FORTY-FIVE
A Strange Acceptance Speech

Today, I look back in amazement at the ample and constructive time I was able to give to my career at Provident Home Life Insurance Company, despite my activities at the School Board and with BPUM. An enormous amount of detail was required in each area, but I was driven by the importance of the entire mission.

I was elected president of Provident Home in the late sixties and while I handled the company's internal legal matters, I hired the late A. Leon Higginbotham Jr., an outstanding attorney, to handle the external matters. Higginbotham, a graduate of Yale Law School, later became the first African-American elevated to the position of Chief Judge of the 3d Circuit Court of Appeals. He also authored the brilliant book entitled "In The Matter Of Color" which exposed the injustices practiced against Black people in the legal process during the Colonial Period. Judge Higginbotham recommended to the United States Senate my appointment to the Board of Directors of the Philadelphia Federal Reserve Bank, on which I served several years.

I remember distinctly the luncheon given to honor me as the first African-American board member in the history of the Federal Reserve System.

In my acceptance speech I said: "America should hang her head in shame at my appointment. The Federal Reserve System was created in 1913 and during the ensuing more than half a century there have been scores of African-Americans much more qualified than I who have been passed over for appointments.

So, that I am the first is not as important as the fact that there must be a remedy to this injustice. There are literally dozens of other important boards in the federal government which have no Black representation. These boards should be looked into and diversified."

I didn't say "Thank you". My acceptance speech was met with frozen silence as I sat down.

The master of ceremonies cleared his throat in embarrassment and remarked to the group, "I believe we should heed the admonishment of Dr. Robinson."

In a few months, Maceo Sloane, CLU, an African-American, was appointed to the Federal Reserve Bank Board of Directors of Richmond, Virginia.

CHAPTER FORTY-SIX
Buried Treasures

As the first African-American board member in the history of the Federal Reserve System, my appointment presented history-making opportunities.

Federal Reserve Bank President David Eastburn asked me to aid him in his quest for racial diversification of employees at the Bank. Toward this effort, he requested that I give a series of lectures on African history to the all-White members of the Board and other top executives. Eastburn also invited to the lecture series the president and vice president of the Evening and Sunday Bulletin, one of Philadelphia's largest newspapers.

I remembered that to change attitudes, the changer has to use emotion to deliver the story. The ideal way is through a motion picture, using subliminal impact. But, not having a film, I put my heart and soul into the series of six lectures as I described the spectacular culture and grandeur our ancestors developed in the West African Songhai Empire between the 8th and 17th Centuries.

When I gave the lectures in 1969, I did not know of the treasures of hundreds of thousands of books and scientific documents in trunks that lay buried deep in the sands around the city of Timbuktu, the most famous city of Songhai. The trunks were found and dug up in the early 2000's.

Had I known, I would have told my Reserve Bank audiences of the foresight of my ancestors to have buried indisputable proof of their world-class literacy and science, suspecting that invaders would tell the lie that our fathers and mothers were illiterate and unsophisticated.

But, even with those facts untold, the impact of the lectures on the Board of Directors was positive.

Board president, Dr. John Coleman, president of Haverford College, asked how he could help to right the terrible wrongs committed against our people. I told him the Europeans robbed our libraries of many very important books. Among them was a set, taken to Morocco, of nine volumes about the Songhai Empire written by Leo Africanus.

Haverford College sent a team to Africa, found the volumes and brought them back to the College, where I not only viewed them, but video-taped sections for my personal library.

The late Reginald Beauchamp, vice president of the Evening and Sunday Bulletin , a noted artist and sculptor, asked what he could do. I told him about

Jenne`, a spectacularly beautiful Songhai  city in the country of Mali. ( I named a grand daughter Jenne` (jah-NAY) after the city and her sister Dara (DAH-rah) after the city's queen mother. Beauchamp secured the particulars from me,verification from the University of Pennsylvania's History Department and built the central portion of the city. The model was complete with homes two- and- three- stories high, banks, tree-lined avenues and the University of Jenne`, which had 1300 professors. Mr. Beauchamp also carved scores of elegantly-dressed tiny figures of people, which he placed in the streets of the city. The model of the city, which measured approximately 1400 square feet, was viewed in the Bulletin's main lobby for several weeks.

When the president of First Pennsylvania Bank saw the model, he requested a showing in the window of the downtown headquarters of the bank. Jenne` was seen by thousands over the next several weeks.

O, what a beautiful city!
O, what a beautiful city!
O, what a beautiful city!
Twelve gates a-to the city, Hallelu!

This spiritual, sung by our fathers and mothers, describes the ancient city of Jenne`, which had twelve gates.

Another history-making event spun off from the lectures was a set-aside of two-and-a-half million dollars for Black contractors, the highest contract in federal building on record, when the Reserve began building a new bank at Seventh and Arch Streets in downtown Philadelphia. In addition, 28% of the building employees were to be Black, although no mention of minority employment took place.

The members of the Board told me this was their effort to right the wrongs done a wronged people.

This gave me added proof of the positive effects of publicizing the grandeur of African history.

HARRIETTE COX ROBINSON, my present wife, is a spirit-filled noblewoman in the image of the queens of the pharaohs of ancient Kemet. A born teacher, now retired after thirty-five ultra successful years in the Philadelphia schools, she continues to counsel, by example, our two daughters and our nine grand, eight great-grand and three great-great-grandchildren.

CHAPTER FORTY- SEVEN
My Bachelor Pad

My first wife, Oren and I were divorced in 1967 and I moved to an elegant, glass-enclosed penthouse apartment at the foot of Chestnut Street in the exclusive Society Hill section of downtown Philadelphia. The Delaware River ran by my bachelor-friendly abode and I spent many nights watching the twinkling riverfront lights and contemplating my future.

One evening, I invited several of my associates from Provident Home in for drinks, bar-b-que and man-talk. My new apartment and the spectacular view of the river were the chief topics of conversation at the get-together. One of my office buddies, after having several martinis, giddily called his wife on the phone and, in an alcoholic haze, gushed excitedly, "You ought to see Ed's new place! He's got wall-to-wall windows from which you can see the biggest damn swimming pool on the planet!"

I decided that if those martinis made him believe the Delaware River was a swimming pool, it was time to switch him to coffee and I duly notified the bartender.

After three years of single life, I decided to search for a "soul mate," a daring adventure not suited for the faint-hearted. Using the power of psychocybernetics,* I conjured up the image of my future wife.

*See explanation, next chapter

Not only would she have the gentleness of spirit, but also a love and honor of our African ancestors. I even called on psychocybernetics to forecast a date she wouldcome into my life.

A few days before the projected date, I received a call from my close friend, the late James East. His sister, Inez, an old classmate of mine, was in town from the West Coast on a quick visit. He wanted to bring her and his ex-sister-in-law, Harriette East, downtown to show off my new apartment and renew old acquaintances.

Shortly after their arrival and my introduction to Harriette, James played my album, "Black Rhapsody". I saw Harriette's eyes fill with tears as my voice told of the beauty, grandeur and sophistication of our Songhai ancestral culture. As I watched her emotional reaction to the recording, I started to feel that psych-cybernetics had led me to a treasured goal. I swear, to this day, that Harriette's drop-dead beauty was only coincidental in my attraction to her.

After six months of dating, we were married. I lost an elegant apartment, but gained the true, lasting love of my life. As of this writing, we will have celebrated our fortieth anniversary.

CHAPTER FORTY-EIGHT
The Goal-Attaining Process

Now that I was happily married and the Ad Hoc Commission of the Philadelphia School District had fulfilled its goal, I could spend more time and energy building Provident Home Life Insurance Company. My position as president brought me into contact with heads of giants in the industry. One of the important things I learned from this interaction, was a program called "Psychocybernetics".

I learned from a book by Maxwell Maltz that psychocybernetics is a program designed to attain goals hitherto seemed unreachable. At a meeting I attended, a head of a general insurance agency reported his agents posted amazing sales results while engaged in the program. He added that although it worked magnificently for his White agents, he couldn't understand why his Black agents were not equally successful.

My research revealed that the attainment of goals depends on being led to success automatically by the part of the brain called the *pre-frontal cortex, which determines positive or negative attitudes*. Further research revealed the pre-frontal cortex of White people determined a love, honor and respect for their European ancestors. On the other hand, the prefrontal-cortex of Black people determine a *lack* of respect, honor or love for their African ancestors. Those positive emotions are *replaced* by feelings of renunciation, shame and disrespect.

The White insurance companies earn billions of dollars because their agents and executives consistently express love and respect for their European customers and those same feelings are returned to the companies in the form of ever-increasing profits.

I decided to teach my agents and executives the undeniable value of knowledge, love and respect for our African ancestors in twice-a-week classes. The first real breakthrough of building our company came from using this psychocybernetics goal-attaining method.

CHAPTER FORTY-NINE
A Giant Step

Of particular interest to me was Penn Mutual, a billion- dollar life insurance company that originated in Pennsylvania. My research disclosed the founders of the company had owned Black captives (erroneously called "slaves") from which they made their original huge wealth.

I wrote the president of Penn Mutual, asserting the immorality of the institution of our captivity and stated there should be some atonement for that transgression.

He suggested I make a presentation to their board of directors, recounting the Company's history and suggesting what "the atonement" should be.

I followed his suggestion and, armed with flip charts and film slides in my presentation , asked for what is called a "surplus note" of $300,000 for "atonement".

A "surplus note" means the money goes into a surplus account without a corresponding liability accounting.

The Penn Mutual Board granted us the money with the stipulation that a member of their board of directors would be invited to sit in on our board meetings to aid us in decision-making. This, of course, we welcomed.

The Penn Mutual executives aided us immensely in what became the spectacular growth of a small Black company.

Our company's goal was to reach three million dollars in assets and thus be attractive to and merge with a Black company that had at least a hundred million dollars in assets.

With the addition of $300,000 to our surplus, our agents were inspired to post unprecedented sales. Our new customer base grew by leaps and bounds. It wasn't long before "suitors" came a'calling, making offers hard to refuse.

We were over two and a half million dollars in assets, far exceeding the million dollar goal I had predicted many years before in Provident Home's dark, smelly basement headquarters. I wryly remembered how my fellow agents howled and fell on the floor with laughter and disbelief at my naive optimism.

One company I had my sights, was North Carolina Mutual Life Insurance Company, of Durham, North Carolina. After several years of "due diligence", we finally merged with North Carolina Mutual, the largest Black business in America at that time in the early Seventies. The president of North Carolina Mutual was my Virginia State College (now University) fellow student, Dr. William Kennedy, who granted me the title of a vice president of the company.

I'm sure all my relatives and neighbors from the Edwin Street of long ago were celebrating in the next life as their "little Eddie" took a giant step.

Psychocybernetics had really worked!

CHAPTER FIFTY
No Time For Coffee

After my retirement from Provident Home and assuming a vice-presidency of North Carolina Mutual Life Insurance Company, I decided to take some time off to catch up on my reading and "smell a little coffee".

That quiet time was short-lived when I received a telephone call from the office of the Governor of Pennsylvania, Milton Shapp. I was advised that Shapp's executive assistant, James Wade, wished to visit me at my home.

I was very excited on meeting Mr. Wade, who revealed the governor wanted to offer me the position of Commissioner of the Bureau of Professional and Occupational Affairs. This was the bureau which licensed about 700,000 Pennsylvanians, including barbers, nurses, doctors and auto dealers–twenty-two professions and occupations in all.

The bureau was under the umbrella of the Department of State, which was headed by the late C. Delores Tucker, an elegant, outstanding Sister. Dr. Tucker was one of the few African-Americans in the newly-elected Shapp cabinet. After speaking with her, (I'm sure that she recommended me for the job), I accepted the position in October, 1975.

The scarcity of Black employees in the bureau's five-hundred person workforce was the result of a long-standing practice of racism. Affirmative action was a thing of the future, but I started my own equality-in-hiring program.

Before I was promoted to the position of executive deputy secretary of the Department of State* twenty five months later, I had increased the percentage of Black employees in the bureau from less than 5% to over 25%. But, more than that, I was able to place a number of Brothers and Sisters into positions to "affirmative action" themselves.

My work at the bureau gave me a "heads up" look at the feelings of entitlement by White people vs. the feelings of unworthiness experienced by Black people.

Out of the 700,000 licensees that the bureau oversaw, an average of 500 complaints were registered by mail and telephone each month. I had the complaints catalogued racially. Only five people, or one percent of the 500 monthly complainants, were Black during the years I assembled the statistics.

It was painfully obvious that Black people suffered many indignities in the State of Pennsylvania, but we seldom heard their complaints. On the other hand,some of the bizarre complaints received from White people spoke to the high level of their feelings of entitlement. *I noted from my bureau experience that it was imperative to raise the feeling of intrinsic (ancestral) worthiness of the Brothers and Sisters to strengthen their demands for justice.*

*The proper name is "Secretary of the Department of the Commonwealth".

CHAPTER FIFTY-ONE
Making Political History

As executive deputy secretary of the Department of the Commonwealth, I became part of a team to raise the level of Black registered voters in the state. Dr. Tucker used her power as Secretary of State to allow registration of voters anywhere in the community. Previously, registration was largely at city halls or other designated sites around the state. I was in charge of North Philadelphia and my nephew, the late David P. Richardson, was responsible for Germantown. The late State Senator Herbert Arlene and the late Father Paul Washington were also members of the registration effort. As a consequence of our efforts, Black Democratic voter registration exceeded White registration by three thousands. Increased Black voter registration led to two history-making events.

In the first event, the late Samuel L. Evans, one of the most influential Black men on the Philadelphia scene for many years, called on William J. Green, a White mayoral hopeful. Evans guaranteed Green an election victory if he would promise to name a Black person as his managing director.

As a result of the strong Black voter registration, Green won the election. He kept his promise to Evans by naming W. Wilson Goode of the Public Utility the first African-American managing director in Philadelphia's history. Goode was Commissioner of the Public Utility Commission of the State of Pennsylvania.

Although the Democrats won the city of Philadelphia, Republicans won the state and Richard Thornburg became the new governor of Pennsylvania.

He promptly appointed Dr. Ethel Allen, a Black physician, as the new Secretary of State and I was kept on as Executive Deputy Secretary of State. A Black man, Barton Fields, was Deputy Secretary of State, which presented Thornburg with a "thorny" problem in 1980. Three Black people were heading what was considered the most powerful department in state government. It did not come as a surprise when Thornburg is reported to have told Dr. Allen, "One of you has to go".

After a friendly discussion between Dr. Allen, Mr. Fields and myself and the realization that I had another income (from North Carolina Mutual), I agreed to leave state government. Dr. Allen wrote me the kindest letter of dismissal in the history of the Commonwealth of Pennsylvania. You can bet that the political move of appointing a White woman to my position allowed the governor to sleep more peacefully at night.

CHAPTER FIFTY-TWO
The White Flip-Flop

Before I recall the second historical event, I'd like to point out my *functional value* to White people and their *intrinsic acceptance* during my tour as executive deputy Secretary of State.

When I first received the appointment, the news traveled swiftly among the three-thousand employees, mostly White. My White colleagues were exceedingly courteous to me in our meetings and made a point to make themselves known and wished me the best when we passed each other on the grounds of the Capitol. It was not lost on them that my position was only two steps below the office of governor.

But, when the word got around that I was fired, those same colleagues dropped me like a venomous spider, *even crossing the street to avoid speaking to me. My value to them was zero because their amygdala had taken over.*

CHAPTER FIFTY-THREE
Police Violence Curbed

The day after I left the office of executive deputy Secretary of State, W. Wilson Goode called and asked me to be an assistant managing director of the city of Philadelphia. I accepted.

Soon after my appointment, there was a siege of police violence against Black Philadelphians. I contacted Morton Solomon, the Police Commissioner, and offered a solution to the increasing number of attacks.

Commissioner gave me an opportunity to make a presentation to the Command Staff of the police department in February, 1980.

I told the top officers of the beauty, grandeur and world-class literacy of the ancestors of Black Americans.

Both the police commissioner and Mayor Green were in awe of the abrupt drop in police violence in the months following the presentation. I was awarded a pictured Certificate of Appreciation, testifying to the presentation's "enlightening, informative and timely contribution". I strongly advised the mayor and police commissioner that one presentation would not be an on-going cure and a series of motion pictures was needed to produce the necessary reprogramming of those responsible for servicing the public.

CHAPTER FIFTY-FOUR
Fairness Rejected

W. Wilson Goode, the new managing director, was a fascinating character study. His affable outward demeanor in no way revealed his razor-sharp intellect or his attention to detail. A graduate of Morgan State University and the University of Pennsylvania, he could skim through a thick document and be totally cognizant of its contents.

Stern, but brilliant, he also had a religious side (he later became a Baptist minister) and was known to kindly admonish persons who uttered the salty words of anger or frustration sometimes heard in City Hall corridors

My first assignment from Goode was the director of the Department of Records, a large department suffering from both low morale and performance. By calling on psychocybernetics, along with the extensive massaging of egos of the numerous centers of influence in the department, I was able to lift both morale and performance in just one year.

My next assignment was to create a bureau which would have as its purpose the increase of contracts to minority contractors. I invented the name Minority Business Employment Council, or MBEC, for short.

As Executive Director of MBEC, I had to first develop a fail-safe process to certify whether the applicant was indeed a "minority". The process had to be applicable to the guidelines of the Federal government.

Incidentally, we were awarded "The Best Certification Process For Minority Contractors In the United States" in 1980.

Meanwhile, I notified the several organizations of minority contractors that they had to become "certified" by MBEC as minority contractors before they could bid on or obtain contracts through the city.

I was assigned a huge office, large enough to accommodate a work-force which included secretaries, inspectors, and accountants. As applicants for awards of city contracts flooded into our office, we were required to follow federal guidelines as to the definition of "minority". I never saw so many thin-nosed, white-skinned, straight-haired contractors swearing they had suddenly become Black or Indian.

They were aware the new directions were to award fifteen percent of federal-funded and state -funded contracts to minority contractors.

My percentage aim for the City of Philadelphia was much *higher: I mandated 38 percent to match the Black population of the city.*

The White contractors went *ballistic!* Their rage was fueled by the threatened end to a racist system that had provided their companies *with practically all of the contracts for generations on end!* They had no intentions of giving up that bonanza without a fight-to-the-death! In my talks with the White contractors, they tried to validate their inherent belief that their "whiteness" entitled them to one-hundred percent of the contracts. The terms "fairness" and "a piece of the pie" did not exist in their racist vocabulary.

CHAPTER FIFTY-FIVE
The "New Minority"

The White contractors took their rage to the White-dominated courts, hoping that "their" judges would strike down the "insane" idea that Black contractors deserved a piece of the federal and state contracts pie.

John Macklin, my extraordinarily competent executive assistant, obtained and documented proof from the city's computers that Black contractors had obtained *only nine-tenths of one percent* of city contracts in the three years prior to 1980.

This was all the proof our allies in Philadelphia City Council needed to get passed legislation requiring that a *minimum of fifteen percent* of city contracts be awarded to minority contractors.

White contractors, while losing that specific case, tried an "end-around" play to further dilute the Black contractors' pool by having White women contractors classified as "minority". Then, the White contractors transferred 51% of their firms' assets to their wives and tried to pass their companies off as "minority."

I responded by having MBEC inspectors stringently examine the competency of wives in their husbands' businesses. In this way, I was able to thwart many of the bogus "minority" White women contractors.

The battle is still being waged all over the United States, as each MBEC, (some cities have different names), struggles to get a fair share of federal and state contracts.

Goode next assigned me to create a bureau within the Philadelphia Housing Authority to certify minority contractors for a share of the hundreds of millions of building, maintenance etc. dollars. The names differed but the battles were the same. White contractors were steadfast in their opposition to giving up their nearly 100% dominance.

I diligently fought against that racist policy until my retirement in 1985.

A few years later, the power of increased Black voter registration was felt for the second time. Again, the hard work of a few of us in 1979, which increased Black Democratic registration to surpass Whites', manifested itself. This time, Philadelphians elected their first African-American mayor: The Honorable W. Wilson Goode!

CHAPTER FIFTY-SIX
Africa Today

The year is 1980. I joined a group of Philadelphians as we boarded a plane to New York, the first stop of our maiden trip to West Africa, the ancestral home of most African Americans. Our final destination was Senegal and aside from what we were able to glean from travel brochures and informational meetings, we didn't have a clue what to expect.

As the plane neared Senegal, I couldn't help but feel a rising surge of excitement as I looked out the window. "The land of my fathers and mothers", I thought. "And I'm the first of my family to return since Grandmother Nzinga was brought to Trenton, N.J. in 1813".

It was only a short time, but it seemed like an eternity before my feet touched the sacred soil of Mother Africa. An indescribable feeling swept over me, starting from my feet and coursing upward to the crown of my head.

Did you ever see glass vibrate when a certain high note is played on a violin? Well, that's how my insides vibrated when the territorial imperative operated for me.

I was actually standing on ancestral soil!

But my ecstasy was short circuited and I was shocked by many of the sights I saw. I could not believe the signs advertising skin lightening. Likewise, I was appalled seeing the blond and orange-colored wigs and weaves on the heads of richly-hued sisters.

It wasn't difficult to discover where the anti-Black brainwash was coming from. American films, translated into French, were showing everywhere. I knew that I would have to bring my problem-solving motion pictures to Africa and everywhere Americanized films were shown.

On the positive side of our trip, I was excited to see on the streets everywhere people who looked like my people in America but attired in the regal robes of our ancestors.   In the market place, women were the entrepreneurs and they displayed their jewelry, art , clothing, woven baskets and other artifacts like the professionals they were.

I marveled how erect and proud the people on the streets carried themselves. I took time to view the beautiful Senegal University and walked its marble hallways with excitement.

The buildings and shops in Dakar, the capital city of Senegal, were as modern and busy as any we saw in metropolitan America. A modern bus drove up to take us to our beautiful hotel in the suburbs of the city, about twenty minutes away. After a wonderful supper in the dining room, we danced to all the latest tunes played by an expert musical quintet. We became "instant Senegalese" as we joined the dancers on the floor because we instinctively knew the rhythms and steps recognized by Black folks around the world.

CHAPTER FIFTY-SEVEN
Indescribable Horror

By far my most heart-wrenching African experience, was my trip to Goree Island, a small island off the coast of Senegal. It is surrounded by deep water which allowed large ships to come close to shore.

On the island was a large building with a series of dungeons on the ground floor. Our captured mothers and fathers were kept in these dungeons for weeks on end, waiting to be sold.

Each dungeon was only large enough to accommodate approximately forty people, but the White captors crammed two to three times that many of our ancestors in that small space. There were no toilets in the dungeons, so our ancestors were forced to relieve themselves where they stood, laid, or sat. *Human feces and waste kept piling up month after month and year after year, for over two hundred years. Disease killed many thousands of our forefathers, mothers and their children.*

There was one door leading from the dungeons to the dock. Above the door, written in large letters were the words, "Door Of No Return". The African captives who survived the hell of the dungeons were boarded onto a good-sized skiff, which took them to a larger sailing vessel. There they were loaded onboard for the voyage to a new hell–The Americas.

CHAPTER FIFTY-EIGHT
Human Shark Food

As I stood looking out the "Door Of No Return", I recalled, from my years of study and numerous accounts, the horror of what happened next: Our ancestors were packed in below the decks of the ship and shackled, lying down, with scarcely three inches between them. To carry as many captives as possible, there were as many as three tiers of humanity. The waste material excreted from the captives on the top tiers rained down on those on the bottom tiers.

Again, disease was rampant and as soon as it was discovered, the captors threw our fathers, mothers, sisters and brothers overboard, dead or alive. This horrific episode was known as the "Era of the Fat Sharks," because the huge, waiting fish never went without a feeding day for over two hundred years.

The top layer of the bottom of the ocean is covered with the skeletons of the citizens of the fabulous Songhai Empire. It is not well known that, in years past, a convoy of ships went out from New York to the middle of the Atlantic Ocean and reverently dropped a steel monument to pay homage to our African ancestors who perished at sea.

My studies also revealed that as the African captives were unloaded at the numerous Southern ports, the babies were taken from the arms of their parents and raised separately. As a result, the offspring would never learn their city or country of origin and that their African ancestors were of world-class literacy and science.

Under the harsh, dehumanizing tutelage of their White captors, the babies would be taught they were personally inferior, their features and color were badges of degradation and their native land was a dangerous, uncivilized jungle.

In addition, a White Jesus might accept them, _in spite of their color_, if they obeyed, imitated, protected and revered their White "masters".

Sadly, the majority of present day African-Americans are struggling under the crippling burden of the same brainwash.

All of these things came to me as I stood on Goree Island with tears in my eyes.

CHAPTER FIFTY-NINE
Back In America

It is the summer of 2011 and I am in front of "The President's House," located a short distance from the so-called "Liberty Bell" in downtown Philadelphia.

"The President's House" became the first White House in 1790 when President George Washington, today hailed as "The Father of Our Country," moved into the mansion with 15 White servants and 9 Black captives.

The mansion was a gift from financier Robert Morris, whose immense wealth came from the money earned literally from the blood, sweat, tears and lives of chained Songhai West Africans and their descendants.

Washington lived at the mansion from 1790 to 1797 and forced the captives to labor there endlessly. They were raped, sodomized and beaten.

The height of shameless hypocrisy was the fact that the captives were housed behind a stable for horses, which was situated just five feet from the present entrance to the center for the Liberty Bell. To heap insult upon outrage, the Liberty Bell is inscribed with these words: "Proclaim liberty throughout all the land unto all the inhabitants thereof."

In the 1700s, Black people were considered as "property," that is, something to be "owned." Three hundred years later, Cleveland, Ohio Black basketball star LeBron James had the vicious cries of "traitor" hurled at him when he decided to make an independent decision about his playing future. I wonder how much of that "property" attitude still exists today?

CHAPTER SIXTY
Captives In The White House

In 2003, the city of Philadelphia and the National Park Service took control of converting the remnants of Morris mansion into a tourist attraction in the Liberty Bell area. As soon as the announcement was made, an activist organization, led by Michael Coard, an exciting young attorney, took on the ambitious task of *Honoring the African Captives Of President George Washington At America's First White House*. I became involved because of my passion to change the programmed misconceptions of Black ancestry believed by millions who would visit the area. In addition, I was intrigued by the organization's goals and name –Avenging The Ancestors Coalition, with the acronym ATAC, (pronounced ATTACK). I was honored to be considered the Elder/Consultant of the group.

Our team, which included the architectural firm of Walter Livingston, contacted the city President's House Supervising Committee countless times with requests that the Black captives be respectfully recognized in the mansion restoration exhibit.

Ignored by federal, state and city governments, ATAC demonstrated in the streets around Sixth and Market , demanding that information be included in the model revealing that the ancestors of African-Americans came from beauty, grandeur and sophistication of world-class literacy.

Finally, Attorney Coard got the proper replies to our letters and meetings got under way.

Twenty-one firms submitted models of the restored mansion in the huge auditorium of the Philadelphia Convention Center. *Only our model revealed the sophistication of the captives' ancestry*.

I asked many viewers of the models, including White college students, this question: "From what type of culture did the ancestors of the nine African captives come?"

Every person, _including Black viewers_, gave one or more of the following answers: "Jungle, savage, bestial, illiterate, unsophisticated."

Needless to say, our architectural/activist team didn't even score in the top five among the bidders.

I was asked to become a consultant to a White Washington, D.C. team that had no problem showing pictures of our true Songhai history in its final restoration bid.

But the goal of honor and respectability was completely destroyed when the Songhai ancestry highlight was rejected by the Supervising Committee, made up of the Mayor's appointees. Ironically, the mayor and the bid-winning architectural firm, which also rejected mention of Songhai ,were African-American.

Finally, in early 2011, the First President's House opened with great fanfare and news coverage, but nothing of the grandeur and literacy of the ancestors of the captives was exhibited. As of now, millions of Liberty Bell Center visitors will go away with the distorted picture of savagery, cannibalism and stupidity of African-American ancestors.

CHAPTER SIXTY-ONE
Terrorists In America

While Americans are concerned about terrorist attacks from other countries, we African-Americans must be concerned about attacks on us from White hate groups here at home.

In January, 2011, a neo-Nazi was arrested with dozens of homemade grenades with which he planned to bomb a Dr. Martin Luther King parade in Spokane, Washington.

The number of Anti-Black hate groups has exploded from 602 in the year 2000, to 1002 in 2010 and the number of anti-Black incidents have sky-rocketed to nearly 200,000 according to the Southern Poverty Law Center. The Center, based in Montgomery, AL, has kept track of the rise of hate groups for generations.

The reason for the dramatic rise in hate activity, according to the Center, "is based on the furious rhetoric from the political right aimed at the country's first Black President–a man who has come to represent …on-going changes in the racial makeup of this country."

As an African elder, I feel that I have a duty to expose the alarming growth rate of anti-Black activity in America. *It is my hope that when people of good will are warned of the people of ill intent , the negative direction of race relations will be reversed.*

You can get crucial information about American hate groups and their web sites by sending for "The Special Issue-Intelligence Report" published by the Southern Poverty Law Center, 400 Washington Ave., P.O. Box 5832, Montgomery, AL, 36177-7459.

AHMED BABA was the last president of the Timbuktu-based Sankore (Without Equal) University. He was considered one of the top three intellectuals of the Sixteenth Century. Thousands of Europeans and other races studied at his feet at the university. He authored forty-five books now housed in Mali in the Ahmed Baba Institute and Museum, which also contains twenty-five thousand books of the Treasures of Timbuktu. Captured by Caucasians, Baba and other intellectuals were imprisoned in Morocco for over twenty years.

CHAPTER SIXTY- TWO
Change Necessary

After spending enormous amounts of time and energy making over three thousand African history presentations over the last 70 years, I have come to a major conclusion concerning the lack of impact on the lessening of ills that plague Blacks . *We have to change the vehicle for the delivery of our message.*

We are thrilled by the change of attitude and behavior of the thousands we did reach, *but there has been no positive impact on the vast majority of people, Black or White.*

In fact, Blacks killing Blacks, the major indicator of worsening ills, has increased from one every two weeks in the Sixties to more than two-hundred-eighty every two weeks in 2011.

What is the answer?

We say FILM. Not just any old film or "Huxtable Family" viewings , but a series of expertly and beautifully photographed dramatic movies revealing the beauty, grandeur and sophistication of 16th century Songhai.

The scientific reason for this series is to concentrate on the basic problem of African-Americans and Blacks around the world– the brainwash against our ancestral worthiness (see page 61).

A dramatic example of the power of film is to witness how the media has been used in recent years to convince Americans to hate Russia, Germany, China and Japan, only to teach tolerance and love of the same countries when it became economically convenient.

I am convinced that we can be equally effective in using film to provide the antidote to anti-Black fear and contempt, thus turning the tide of racial injustice.

I have carefully crafted four movie scripts, which I thought the world, especially my people, would welcome with open arms.

Hooking up with videographer Bob Lott, we began seeking wealthy people in the arts, business, sports and law as sponsors "to save lives and create racial understanding."

Here are two of the typical responses we received:

From a film-maker: "I'm not interested in solving social problems. I'm only interested in making money!"

From a White legislator : "If White kids were killing each other as Black kids are and someone like you came along with a *possible* solution, we'd be literally throwing money at your project! You see, we *love* our children."

We have tried every angle to get the film project off the ground, but the primary interest shown for Black films are those movies that reinforce the anti-Black brainwash. I have not found the angle that will open the doors of healing film production.

There has to be a way. I will search for it as long as there is breath in my body.

CHAPTER SIXTY-THREE
Fact And Fiction

During the last several decades, I've been analyzing the causes of White America's contempt and/or fear of Black people. I've found that the negative feelings usually go one way—non-Blacks against Blacks. The Black reaction to the contempt or fear is just that—a reaction. Black people are programmed from infancy to feel positive about nearly everything white, including and especially people.

In addition to the inherent amygdala, the contempt and/or fear of Black people is based on a number of *myths,* which I hope to dispel here by logic and documentation. Hopefully, this chapter will help us to undertake the seemingly uphill battle for truth, unity and cultural understanding.

The following statements and research are based on the knowledge of there being no absolutes, but generally speaking, the information can be substantiated. If you have doubts, take some time to observe where you shop, live or go to school.

There are several categories of the contempt and/or fear:

FICTION: The Emancipation Proclamation (EP) freed Black people from "slavery."

FACT: The so-called Emancipation Proclamation was a farce that freed no one. The freedom of captives in the Southern States would have had to be enforced by Confederate soldiers, who obviously refused to do so.

The real purpose of the EP was to overturn the laws of the Black Code, which prohibited Black people from serving in the armed forces. A presidential proclamation was "warranted by the Constitution upon military necessity." The "military necessity" was the North was losing the war.

Over a half-million Black people participated on the side of the North in their freedom fight. Included were 217,00 soldiers and sailors, who fought in 204 battles, winning 21 Congressional Medals of Honor.

Here are two fascinating facts of Black participation in the war against the South which are previously unknown; 300,000 Black folks built the bridges, roads and fortifications used by the Northern armies. In addition, they acted as espionage agents, one of which was the major conductor of the *Underground Railroad*, Harriet Tubman.

Captives in the house would send war secrets heard to women outdoors, who transmitted the information by a predetermined way of hanging clothes on lines in the plantation fields. That information could then be transmitted to the Union forces by drum or by spirituals, our message songs.

 At the conclusion of the War Between the States, (erroneously labeled the Civil War), President Lincoln and his generals acknowledged that the *huge numbers of Black men who bravely bore arms actually won the war for the North.*

France also recognized this as fact by creating and presenting to the United States the Statue of liberty in 1885. Now you know why the majestic statue that towers over Ellis Island was presented with the following words:

"In commemoration of a captive people, who, for the first time in history, freed themselves."

FICTION: The fear and/or contempt of Black people by White people is a conditioned reflex.

FACT: The amygdala triggers alarm and fear when it sees someone of a different race (see TIME magazine, October 20, 2008).

FICTION: The ancestral home of most African-Americans was a jungle.

FACT: Their ancestral home was the West African Songhai Empire, which was made up of university cities, iron and steel factories, beautiful homes and tree-lined avenues.

FICTION: The African-American homeland was void of literary sophistication.
FACT: In the early decade of 2000, thousands of trunks, buried 400 years earlier, were found around the city of Timbuktu. The trunks, filled with books, manuscripts of science, medicine and law treatises of literature, proved the world-class literacy of African-American ancestors.

FICTION: Black people are poor.
FACT: African-Americans spend $900 billion dollars a year, a sum that exceeds that of Canada and three other countries. Unfortunately, $120 billion is spent on hair products, cars, clothes and food, and only $40.5 billion on health, insurance education and books. (Source: Target Market News and the Selig Center for Economic Growth).

FICTION: Blacks are less intelligent than Whites.
FACT: According to the *Association for the Advancement of Science*, headquartered at Yale University in its 1996 Series, Blacks in America are 150% smarter than Europeans. This analysis is based on the measurements of the DNA Series of both groups. The greater the number of the DNA Series, the greater the probability of genius. Blacks in America have nine DNA Series, as compared to Europeans, who only have six. The chimpanzee has five.

FICTION: There is no proof of African ancient literacy and mathematical knowledge.
FACT #1: A nine-thousand-year-old vase was discovered in Ancient Egypt (Kemet) with the words "fraction one-half" inscribed on it. The first book by Europeans (Homer) wasn't written until more than six-thousand years later.

FACT#2:   Pages of the creation of algebra 3700 years ago in Ancient Egypt by a Black African, Ahmes, can be found in his book in the British Museum today. Europeans didn't find out about algebra until about 1500 years later, according to the *World Book Encyclopedia.*

FICTION: Blacks are more violent than Whites.
FACT: Europeans are the most violent and aggressive of all races, according to the 15th Edition of Encyclopedia Britannica, page 600. Also, *The Iceman Inheritance,* by Michael Bradley, documents the wars and killings of the last five centuries attributed to the White race.

FICTION: Blacks are closer to the ape in evolution.
FACT: Color of skin; Chimpanzees and
Whites: White.
Type of hair; Chimpanzees and Whites:
Straight, undeveloped.
Blacks: Tightly curled, developed.
Infestation of hair; Chimpanzees and
Whites: Head lice.
Blacks: No head lice.
Bodily hair; Chimpanzees and Whites:
Profuse. Blacks; Scant.
Facial features: Chimpanzees and
Whites; Thin lips, narrow noses,
close-set eyes, large ears.
Blacks: Full lips, broad noses, wide-set
eyes, small ears.
Bodily build: Chimpanzees and
Whites: long bodies, short legs,
undeveloped buttock muscles.
Blacks:–short bodies, long legs,
developed buttock muscles.

The information above is not an attempt to make White people feel badly. The untruths, fear and contempt fostered by Whites against Blacks through the centuries has been used to justify the astronomical profits earned by the captors on the blood, sweat, tears and lives of our mothers and fathers.

Herein, to my knowledge, is the first time the denunciations of Black people have been answered in a comprehensive way.

CONCLUSION

A very important goal is to align the human standard of beauty with the standard of beauty in other forms of nature.

For example, when we look at a bouquet of flowers, we are enchanted by the colors, shapes, fragrances and *differences* of each flower. Some people might believe the lily is beautiful, but the lily does not set the standard of beauty for the rest of the flowers in the bouquet. The same people might find the black orchid, the red rose or the yellow chrysanthemum equally beautiful.

Why, then, does the European color, facial features and hair set the standard of beauty for all other races? What must be done to align the multi-standard of floral beauty with the varied array of human beauty? What must be done for America to experience the same intensity of beauty in the face, color and shape of a Whoopie Goldberg as in the face, color and shape of a Beyonce`?

Fortunately, I have arrived at that point in my human-floral appreciation development.

For years I looked at the pictures of African-appearing ancestors of ancient Egypt (Kemet) and the Songhai Empire. I associated each picture in my mind of the world map of DNA series which put the African people far ahead of all other races in probabilities of genius.

In addition, I studied the results of racial comparisons of accomplishments in every area of track and field and all other sports.

I studied the works of the great chemist, (Mr.) Carol Barnes, who made the break-through discovery of the chemical make-up of melanin, which has the same chemical components of fragrant perfumes. This explained why there was a significant greater pleasantness in the aroma of richly pigmented (dark) people than in poorly pigmented (light) people.

I researched the insecticides sold on the market to combat breakouts of head lice (genus Mallophagga) in the heads of people with straight hair.

Doing all of these things, as well as teaching and writing about them, successfully overcame the programming of a communications media designed to degrade African intrinsic (ancestral) value and our physical characteristics.

Now, for the big question: How can America and the world put the "right train" of education, financial stability, corrective African and American history, employment and definitions of physical beauty on the "right track" of universal honor and respect?

The solution is difficult and surprising. With apologies to Malcolm "X" and other doubting people of color, White people are not inherently evil. I found that difficult to believe after suffering so many years of racial injustice. But it is truth that will finally set us all free.

My scientific research revealed that all people have a growth in their brain that developed several million years ago. The walnut-sized growth, called the amygdala developed when there was critical value in instantly distinguishing those "others" from those who nurture and protect you.   The alarm immediately sounds off and the reaction is fear, flight or driving the "intruder" away.

Human beings, as we know them, are aware of the future, so the amygdala not only sounds an alarm to drive off current threats, but also seeks to extinguish future ones. This can mean trying to eradicate an entire group that poses danger. The signal is difficult to disconnect. This is why there is the current danger of Black eradication explained in the chapter on the growth of White terrorist organizations in America.

In a 1990 Harvard study, psychologist and social scientist Mahzarin Banaji co-created what is known as the implicit association test (IAT), which explored the instant connections the brain draws between races and traits. This test, which is available on line (www.implicit.harvard.edu), asks people to pair pictures of

White or Black faces with positive words like *joy, love, peace and happy or negative ones like agony, evil, hurt and failure*. Speed of choice is important since the survey explores automatic associations. When respondents are told to link positive traits to Whites and undesirable traits to Blacks, the choices were almost instant. When Whites were labeled failures and Blacks exalted as glorious, the choices slowed considerably, a sure sign the brain was struggling.

When Banajji and neuroscientist Liz Phelps introduced brain scans of the subjects, the MRI disclosed that when White people were shown Black faces, there was significantly greater activation of the amygdala, proving the critical function of the gland is *fear conditioning*.

Black people also have the amygdala, but man developed two types of cortexes hundreds of thousands of years later. When these cortexes are programmed to believe positive things about the "others," that is, people who do not look like the family or tribe, the amygdala's alarm system is shut off.

The reason Whites aren't shunned and feared by Blacks is because Black folks are programmed from birth to associate the color white with all things positive. *The ninety-nine synonyms children learn for white are positive. Of one hundred twenty-four synonyms children learn for black, one hundred twenty-three are negative. Their first cartoons and films teach children to love and embrace everything white.*

The films with the most impact highlight the beauty and grandeur of the European land of ancestry, i.e. . "King Arthur and the Knights of the Roundtable" for the English, "Julius Caesar" for the Italians, "Napoleon" for the French, etc.

These and similar films unleash a powerful force called the *Territorial Imperative, which states you cannot reach the heights of your creative or intellectual potential unless you love, honor and respect the people and land of your ancestry.*

The Territorial Imperative is so powerful, some creatures, like the salmon, cannot reproduce until they return to the place of origin. This fish must swim hundreds of miles upstream against a raging current, dodging the grasp of hungry bears in order to spawn the next generation of salmon.

Conversely, not only do African Americans *not* learn about their majestic Songhai Empire ancestry, White people have thrust jungle, savagery and ugliness into their ancestral memory vacuum .

 To summarize, the *Black amygdala's alarm system has been shut down because of continuous positive programming of White ancestral ingredient.* Conversely, the White amygdala alarm system has *not been shut down because there has been no positive, consistent programming of Black ancestral ingredient.* A four-week celebration of a parade of *African American personalities in February doesn't even begin to provide the programming necessary.* Although the amygdala plays an important role in the racism practiced against African Americans, there are other factors which create psychological violence practiced against Black people all over the world.

Some of these factors are the result of two-and-a-half centuries of Black captivity (so-called slavery). That captivity stands alone in all of recorded history as the most horrific of all evilness practiced against a people.

The negative results of that era, instead of diminishing as time goes by, have increased over the past one hundred forty-six years.

In order to insure the permanence of the ever-increasing trillion-dollar profits made from African captivity, the essential goal of White plantation owners was to *de-humanize the Black family*. This diabolical scheme was instituted in the mid 1600's by passing the first of the *Black Codes, with the aim of destroying the Black man as the family's protector and provider. All of the big plantation owners subscribed through the years to at least four periodically-issued manuals. The manuals provided the owners strategies and the most effective way to enforce the codes.*

These manuals are available on the internet to study

today. They are *The American Farmer, The Farmer's Register, The Southern Agriculturist and The American Planter and Soil of the South.*

Here are examples of the diabolical strategies:

"It is more profitable to work a Black man so hard that he dies and then with the profit buy another captive."

"Cut the Black man off from any knowledge of his world-class Songhai Empire by taking the babies away from the parents as soon as they arrive from Africa."

Proof that this implementation was successful is that few, if any, African Americans know the African country or city from which their ancestors were brought.

These techniques were designed in the Black Codes specifically to annihilate the Black man as protector and provider for his family:

"Make it punishable by death for a Black man to defend his wife or daughter against a White man's rapacious intent."

"To strike a White man, except in defense of the Black man's captor, is a crime punishable by death."

"Any crops or goods owned by a Black man belong to and can be seized by his captor."

Even after so-called "freedom," these codes were made stricter each generation by a limited employment market, job discrimination and a racist justice system.

Today, because of intense conditioning, the African American man stands the most powerless of family men in his role of protector and provider. This conditioning has caused the destruction of respect for him by his wife and children. Black boys have no strong male role model. These boys grow up, marry and their marriages are faced with the same conditional deficiencies. And so the vicious cycle worsens. The breakup of Black families lowers the respect of Black people by Whites and thus increases the contempt, a salient element of racism.

Here is the bottom line: The *real problem facing Black people of the world is that everyone has been programmed by the drama of the communications media to despise both the culture of West African ancestry and the physical appearance of African Americans. This conditioning adds to the genetic disposition from the amygdala of White people to fear and dislike Black people. This inherent disposition of fear is reinforced because Black people are most removed in physical appearance from Whites.*

It is impossible for even a thousand pictures of African American heroes during February to put the African American History "train" on the "right track." This is because the "right track' is Songhai and ancient Egyptian (Kemetan) history.

Only the subliminal beauty, grandeur and sophistication of dramatic motion pictures of the Songhai Empire during the 15th and 16th Centuries can affect the amygdala and change the negative attitudes of the world toward present-day African Americans.

EPILOGUE

Messages From My Family

TO MY HUSBAND
When Two Became One

Little did I know that when I enrolled in a ten-week in-service course in African-American History, sponsored by the School District of Philadelphia, that my whole life would be transformed.

I saw you as an instructor, handsome, intelligent, knowledgeable, one whose dynamic presentation was mesmerizing. Your voice echoed the rhythm of ages past–one which took us across great turbulent waters to the mighty kingdoms of our motherland, Songhai, West Africa.

As an elementary school teacher, I realized how "miseducated" I was. You awakened a new horizon, a new purpose and responsibility for me to embrace the greatness of my African heritage. I accepted the challenge to tell my first grade students that they were descendants of kings and queens.

What a joy it was to witness my youngsters standing proud, walking with dignity and pride as they created African homes, banks, schools and beautifully dressed people.

Imagine walking in Center City and hearing someone call out "Teacher! Remember me? *I* was Queen Nzinga in your play. I am now an attorney here in Philadelphia.

Thank you for teaching me my history!"

Was it 'happenstance," or most assuredly "God-stance," that a classmate of yours from Virginia State University, the late Inez East Dones, came from California to Philadelphia to visit her brother, the late James East. She was anxious to see you and to spend some time with me, her sister-in-law.

Well, as the story goes, we were invited to your fabulous apartment in the Society Hills Towers.

But, the unbelievable happened. You did not remember that I was a student of yours in a ten-week African History course. I sat on the on the first row, first seat. The story gets better. You and my former husband, the late Melvin East, sang in a men's chorus together. I attended every concert and every party.

And that's not all. I invited you to be guest speaker at an awards banquet at my church.

Need I say more?

The story unfolds into a "symphony of love." We were married forty years ago, on June 9th, 1971.

I thank my God for giving you to me. You walk with dignity and pride , like the music of "Pomp and Circumstance." You gently soothe and calm my spirit like a lullaby. When a situation demands immediate attention, you move with the power of the "Prelude In C# Minor." Your passion for wanting to solve the problems facing African peoples throughout the world gives rise to songs of courage and inspiration as in the song, "Ride On, King Jesus, No Man Can-A Hinder Me." As your songs take flight, you bring harmony and melody to a new horizon and a new vision of the greatness of our African ancestors.

My love, you know my needs, my hopes, my dreams and my desires. You take a genuine interest in all that I do. Your heart is generous, kind, forgiving and full of compassion. You have made a home out of a house by being thoughtful and kind. You are full of true wisdom and strength. You are someone whose love I will always cherish.

My wish for you is the fulfillment of your dream, the production of the motion picture, "Whispers of the Medallion."

Love,

From One Of Two Who Have Become One,

Your Wife,

HARRIETTE COX ROBINSON

Whom Do Men Say You Are:

You Are The Keeper Of The Keys To Our History.
You Are The Scholar With An African Mission.
You Are An International Scholar, Curriculum Pioneer,
Renowned Author, Successful Entrepreneur, A Proud African, A
Legendary African-American Historian.

* * *

CALVIN & ELAINE ROBINSON, your brother and sister.

You exemplify our family strength through your achievements and unselfishness. Our ancestors are proud of your untiring dedication to weave together the golden threads of our glorious African history.

* * *

NATHAN HARMON, your grandson, age 28.

Grandpop Ed, you are a mentor, educator, revolutionary and visionary. Throughout your life you have striven to teach the world who African people are and from whence we came. More importantly, you have spread the legacy of the sophistication and brilliance of African genesis to your grandchildren and family at large.

From a young age, I have vivid memories of pictures of the universities, beautiful homes and tree-lined streets of Songhai, our ancestral home. In my mind I have images of our great mothers and fathers adorned in the finest silks and golden jewelry, wearing masterfully wrought leather shoes.

I am filled with pride as I hear how our ancestors led the world in literature, agriculture, mathematics and many other trades of modernity and civilization.

I hold dearly the legacy of my name, Askia, which I share with Askia Mohammad, one of the great emperors of the Songhai Empire during the 15th century.

Our family has been better able to achieve our God-given potential because you have armed us against the onslaught of negative programming of all things African and the eradication of our true history.

Your life, which is dedicated to lowering the disproportion societal ills of Black people, is a true testament to the benefits of intrinsically knowing, owning and honoring our ancestors.

God bless you, Grandpop Ed.

* * *

RUSSELL ROBINSON, your grandson, age 30.

My father, Edward W. Robinson III, died when I was only 8 years old, but I remember the long talks we had about the African history that I would not be taught in school. He continued to remind me that I am a descendant of the Songhai Empire and I should not allow the negativity of others to distract me.

My mother, Phyliss, continued to reinforce the advantage of knowing "who you are" historically , while raising me as a single parent, not always the easiest task.

Granpop Ed, your counseling was invaluable as I tried to make it out of the fog called my teenage years. You reminded me of the strength we inherited as a people from such geniuses as Imhotep, the African father of scientific medicine.

In school, there were no lessons on the greatness of Africa. When I asked about the inclusion of European history and the exclusion of my history, I was either ignored or told "that will be covered when you are older." It began to dawn on me that the stories taught by my father, my mother and Grandpop Ed were not just history lessons, but the setting of a bar of possibilities. I began to realize that these were successes I could achieve.

When my Grade Point Average (GPA) dropped to 0.5 in the public school I attended, my mother sent me to a private school and challenged me to get a 3.5 GPA to off-set the lower scores.

You called me on the phone and explained: "What your mother is asking you to do is *expected* of you. Do you think the pyramids were built by people not studying or learning mathematics? That the Greeks came to study in our libraries for no reason?"

Two years later, I left that school with a 3.9 GPA. My grades never faltered again.

I later graduated from Howard University, where I met and married Micala, a beautiful queen who was attending Howard's Law School.

She is now a practicing attorney, I am an investment advisor and we both reflect on the message that you taught us: To know who you are and what you are capable of doing, is powerful enough to help you overcome seemingly unconquerable obstacles.

* * *

PAMELA DIANE JOHNSON, your daughter, age 62.

You have inspired me from childhood with your stories of the grandeur of Songhai, our ancestral home.

* * *

MICHELLE HARMON, your daughter, age 60.

As a child going to school, the teaching focus was on American and World History, excluding any kind of African History except negative images of jungles and huts and our ancestors being dehumanized. These distorted images did nothing to boost my self-esteem, especially since I was attending a predominately White junior high school.

I was empowered to excel as a student after hearing a lecture where "Brother Ed" revealed we are descendants of African queens and kings, among them, Queen Nzinga, Queen Nefertari, Mansu Musa and Imhotep, father of scientific medicine. I became even better equipped to handle being in a hostile environment after learning from "Brother Ed " that our ancestors lived in beautiful cities with tree-lined streets as opposed to boiling frightened bible-toting missionaries in a big iron pot over a roaring fire.

"Brother Ed" became "Papa Ed" after he and my mother married. Now I was getting daily helpings of who I *truly* was, a beautiful African queen, with evolved hair and a richly-pigmented chocolate skin protected by melanin.

Through your teachings and interactions with us as a family, you have taught me how to be successful in marriage, parenting, school, work and just generally coping with the ups, downs and turnarounds of daily life.

As an African-American woman, mother, grandmother and now a retired social worker, I have truly been blessed to have you as a dad, mentor, confidant, African historian, author and trail blazer for all to follow.

I thank God for you, Papa Ed, a shining diamond in my life.

* * *

LUCINDA HARMON, your grand daughter, age 30.

Grandpop Ed, you are the ideal family man, always loving, protective and intelligent. I am amazed by your accomplishments, wisdom and passion to educate our African-American community.

Your history teachings made me a more knowledgeable woman and I am able to enlighten others of the beauty and grandeur of our African ancestry.

I truly believe the truth of our African history will decrease violence and misunderstanding in the world.

Thank you for continuing to be such a supportive person in my life.

* * *

DONALD PATTERSON, your cousin, age 78
JENNYE PATTERSON, your cousin, age 76

We revere you as the elder of our family and salute your world-changing goal of solving the problem of contempt facing African people. We agree that your aim of attitudinal change by a series of motion pictures is the right way to go.

EDUCATIONAL PRODUCTS
PRODUCED BY EDWARD W. ROBINSON, JR.

AFRICAN HISTORY—Teen Summit 1000\
AFRICAN HISTORY *INFUSION* –Philadelphia School District
AFRICAN SCIENCE INFUSION–Philadelphia School District
AFRICAN HISTORY AND SCIENCE TEACHER GUIDES–
Philadelphia School District
TRI-CONTINENTAL TIME LINE
BLACK RHAPSODY—CD
BLACK RHAPSODY MUSICAL
NEW DAY A'COMING—D V D
21ST CENTURY UNDERGROUND RAILROAD—D V D
SONGHAI PRINCESS—D V D
'TWAS THE NIGHT BEFORE KWANZAA—Booklet
FITTEST OF THE FIT—Cassette Tape
RICHARD ALLEN—Video
MOTHER AFRICA–PARTS I AND II—Video
HOW BLACK SOLDIERS WON THE CIVIL WAR—Video
RITES OF PASSAGE—M V D
RITES OF PASSAGE—Manual
LEEDS MIDDLE SCHOOL—Video
WILLIAM PENN HIGH SCHOOL—Video
THE PRIDE AND JOURNEY ANTHOLOGY AND PICTURE GALLERY

FREDERICK L. BONAPARTE, a native of Philadelphia Pa., has enjoyed successful careers in music, journalism, education and business. He credits many of these achievements to his 60-year association with Dr. Robinson, "who convinced me that I could rise to remarkable heights because I have the strength of kings in my wings." Fred retired in 1997 as a senior sales manager with the Bose Corporation, an international leader in audio systems. He now lives in Stone Mountain, GA with his wife, Wendolyn, an elementary school teacher.

DR. EDWARD W. ROBINSON, JR. has worn many cultural hats during his speaking, teaching, researching and singing tours through much of the United States. While revealing the glory and splendor of the ancestry of Black people of the Americas and around the globe, he has found time to be a Pennsylvania state and Philadelphia city official, vice president of a multi-million dollar corporation, earn a doctorate degree in law and be in the forefront of the civil rights struggle in his native Philadelphia.

His 93-year search for the answer to White-on Black hostility is chronicled in *"No Man Can A-Hinder Me."*

Not only does Dr. Robinson expose the hypocrisy of documents like the Constitution and the Emancipation Proclamation, he offers solutions that can be easily undertaken by all oppressed people if they can just overcome the centuries-old "brainwash" of the oppressor.

Dr. Robinson has created many books, films DVD's CD's and curriculums, including *"The Songhai Princess,"* a national award-winning video children's story, co-authored with his wife, Harriette; a television series of historical moments sponsored by the Southland (7-11 Stores) Corporation; and an art gallery consisting of "*The Most Notable Africans and African-Americans;* the *Tri-Racial Comparative Time Line,* a pictured work spanning 22,000 years of European, Asian and African history documented by 37 history books.

He has also produced four film scripts depicting the beauty the beauty, grandeur and sophistication of the ancestral home of African Americans; and an *African Infusion Curriculum* in social studies and science for grades kindergarten through eighth grade for the Philadelphia School District.

Among his numerous awards and citations are the *Martin Luther King Award of the Drum Major for Social Justice and a Founder's Day Keynote Speaker* award in 2007 by the Omega Psi Phi Fraternity (even though he is a member of Alpha Phi Alpha Fraternity); the *2011 Legacy Award of the African*

American Museum of Philadelphia and the *Award of Legacy African-American Historian* by the Institute for the Preservation of African American Music.

He writes of his wife of 40 years, Harriette;

> *As the days hurry down*
> *To a precious few,*
> *The finest thing*
> *I've ever done,*
> *Was loving you.*

Made in the
USA
Columbia, SC